S0-AAD-219

The century of
Dali

The fifty best stories
of Salvador Dali

Jean Christophe
ARGILLET

translated by
Jeffrey Grice

ISBN : 2-915586-30-6
Registered: July 2005
© Timée-Editions July 2005

Printed in Italy

To Sandrine, Loïs and Eve.

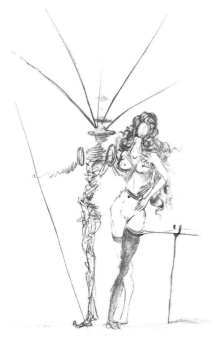

**Frontispiece of the *Apollinaire* series, Dali,
etching, 1966.**

A pproaching Salvador Dali through stories and anecdotes presents no great difficulty to me, for it has been principally from this angle that I have had the honor and privilege of associating with this great genius of the 20th century.

My primal scream at birth was not "D A L I!", but he must have been on the tip of my tongue, for a first memory, told to me much later and which I in turn shall now relate, dates from only two hours after my arrival.

On the 22nd of May 1966, at 2 p.m. to be precise, a certain Pierre Argillet announces, beamingly, the birth of his son to the Divine Dali. The latter, in the process of leaving his apartment at the palatial Paris Hotel Meurice for lunch at Ledoyen on the Champs Elysées, and already in his overcoat, stops in his tracks to ask for a copper plate and a ruby burin. Leaning on his left arm, folded, yet still holding his cane, he engraves the plate, standing all the while. For twenty minutes he incises in this most uncomfortable of positions, a very beautiful couple in very fine detail, later to become the frontispiece of the *Appollinaire* series but originally an improvised gift to a friend and editor, a souvenir to celebrate the arrival of his newborn babe …

Pierre and Geneviève Argillet, my parents, meet Dali in 1959 to commission an original copper engraving for their first illustrated art book. Their admiration for this artist is boundless, and luckily, they hit it off. Twenty years later, this initial illustration for the *Poetic Incantation*, has given way to some two hundred others, and the Argillet couple rank, thanks as much to the quality as to the quantity of subjects treated, as the top editor of the artist's engravings. My father's Roleiflex camera, often within reach in reminiscence of his young reporter days, is also allowed to immortalize on film several exceptional moments spent with the Master.

One immediate consequence of this intensive, long-lasting collaboration was my submersion from the start in the Dali elixir. Not a day went by without Dali's name buzzing in my ears. Much as fairy-tales or fantastic epics are recounted from one generation to the next, I, as a child and adolescent, was brought up on tales of Dali.

Though I must admit, at the time all this left me relatively indifferent. I no more understood the significance of all the engravings stacked in different rooms of the house, than I did the visits of the mustachioed Monsieur with the cane, arriving and leaving in that enormous Cadillac. At the age of six or seven, I was far more interested in playing football with him, or in sprinkling the elegant lady at his side (Gala in her

Introduction

Chanel suit) with the garden hose, deaf to my parents' efforts to pacify me. "Let him be," the Master would say, "it proves he has character."

Finally old enough to realize just who Salvador Dali was, and more than ever keen to approach the personage, it was illness, long agony and finally death that estranged him little by little from my universe. So, unlike my parents who met him in his prime, my impressions of the man stem from childhood memories and from a familiarity with his works and public life, but even more from those dozens and dozens of stories heard over and over again for so long.

Now an art dealer for nearly twenty years and in charge of much of the promotion of Dali's work for the Argillet family, my connection to the great artist has remained unbroken. In the course of exhibitions attended all over the world, I have been able to witness the reactions of a very wide cross section of the public (different age-groups, social conditions and backgrounds) to Salvador Dali and his work.

With these fifty stories, I have tried to highlight the many different facets of his personality, and taken into account questions that interest the public, in sketching a portrait that I hope true to life. In doing so, I deliberately focussed on trustworthy firsthand accounts and sources, and discarded statements often obtrusive and sensational, yet seldom credible.

I wish to extend my warmest thanks to all those who helped me in one way or another in drafting *The Century of Dali*:

Firstly, to all those passionate aficionados still part of the intimate inner "Dalinian" clan: John Peter and Catherine Moore, Robert Descharnes, Marc and Thérèse Lacroix and of course Geneviève Argillet, my mother, all of whom enabled me, through this passion that unites us, to revive all these souvenirs and images.

Secondly, to all those gone to join their idol but who, through their writings and stories, were of precious help to me in evoking Salvador Dali: Reynolds Morse, Albert Field, Joseph Forêt, Louis Pauwels, Phyllis Lucas, Pierre Roumeguere and of course, Pierre Argillet, my father.

Thirdly, many thanks to all those whose enthusiasm (Dalinians are never lukewarm) has now allowed a fitting French homage to be paid to the Master in this, the centenary of his birth: Christophe Barge, Laurent Tranier, Yves Jego, Jean Casagran, Jean-Paul Alduy and the town of Perpignan, "the centre of the world." And lastly, many thanks to Jeffrey Grice, Michael Galfer and Diane Pickering for their kind assistance with the English version.

Jean Christophe ARGILLET

Contents

What is the childhood of a genius like? Dali's young years reflect what his life will be. Anti-establishment, blasphemous, he is influenced by a few great personalities, and drawing attention: a prelude to art • • •

1 The young years

" ● ● ● Since nothing can happen worse than death, nothing can happen to me, because I'm already dead" ● ● ●

Dali in the egg by photographer Philippe Halsman, 1942. Halsman and Dali met in 1941 and collaborated until the photographer's death in 1979.

Birth certificates

Salvador Dali does not get off to a normal start in life, with all the conventional smiles, tears and tender loving care. Destiny chose him, by a quirk of fate, perhaps to point out the essential difference between an exceptional human being and an ordinary mortal.

Each of us, if only for the satisfaction of being written somewhere into society, gets a birth certificate … a single one. Salvador Dali has two!

A Salvador Dali Domenech is born in Figueres on the 12th of October, 1901, at 11 a.m., to Salvador Dali Cusi and Félipa Domenech Feres. But, a fact often skipped over by biographers, the infant gives his innocence back to God shortly after, on the 1st of August 1903 at 5 p.m..

This premature death, a tragedy for the Dali parents, is also a source of shame in this small Catalonian village where everyone knows everyone else's business.

So his parents try again, and nine months and barely eleven days after this death, on the 11th of May, 1904 at 8.45 a.m., a second Salvador Dali is born, the one we all know, who will occupy the 20th century for the next eighty-five years.

Dali's father, Salvador Dali y Cusi, a notary in Figueres, around 1904. At the birth of his son, he is forty-one.

As if being of the same sex and Christian name were not enough, Dali's parents are always reawakening to the young Salvador the ghost of his dead brother. This unusual, rather morbid aspect of his upbringing leaves an indelible mark on his character and is an essential key to understanding certain aspects of his work, along with his fantastical, provocative and exuberant personality. Knowing himself to be a double, he has to, so to speak, affirm his uniqueness.

"My father assailed me from birth with a surplus of affection, a love destined not only for me but also for my dead brother, a narcissistic wound that nearly drained my sanity but which my genius managed, thanks to Gala, not so much to heal as to turn to productive ends."

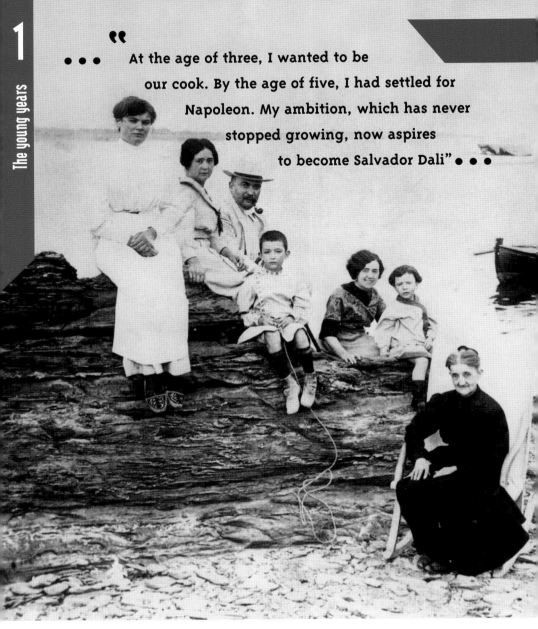

❝
• • • At the age of three, I wanted to be
our cook. By the age of five, I had settled for
Napoleon. My ambition, which has never
stopped growing, now aspires
to become Salvador Dali" **• • •**

The Dali family in 1910. From left to right: Aunt Maria Teresa, Dali's parents, Dali (6 years old),
la Tieta, Ana Maria, the little sister, and Ana, the grandmother.

First pranks

No doubt spurred on by lenient yet overprotective parents, the young Salvador determines to assert himself straightaway. Overly spoiled, mischievous and capricious, sometimes to the point of cruelty, he fast becomes a master at pranks of a dubious nature.

Interestingly enough, Dali's urge to "cuckold," of which he is to boast all his life, is enkindled between the age of five and seven. It is then that he decides to base his social interaction on the systematic use of whim or rebellion against "the society of the others": family, friends, parents, teachers, etc., a society he is never to integrate and will always treat with facetious tricks, becoming himself in the process totally inimitable and impossible to assimilate.

At the age of ten, at the Marist school in Figueres, he already looks "different" with his long blond curls, baggy trousers, shirts with floppy neckties, capes and spats. Sole subscriber in town to *L'Humanité*, he reads all the revolutionary philosophers.

Though he brags about being an "anarchist like Papa," a public notary in Figueres, his portrait of the latter, *The crepuscular old man*, painted at the age of thirteen, is far from flattering. "I often hurt my father. Out of egotism and Jesuitism," he later admits.

Noticing the exaggerated attention his parents pay to his every bowel movement, despite his perfect health, he delights in dissimulating the business from their eyes, searching the house for the most unusual places to hide his stools, the bottom drawers of commodes being a hot favorite.

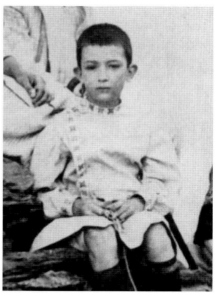

The little Salvador is six years old and "looks" like a model child ...

After parading around the house with an exclamatory "I pooped!", he pretends, when asked where, not to remember so that parents and servants are obliged to inspect every room ferreting for the unthinkable.

"
• • • Salvador Dali Domenech presented himself
for this examination but, when asked to choose three program subjects,
was heard to answer: 'No, none of the teachers of the San Fernando
School have any competence to judge me anyway, and I am
withdrawing.' Certified at the Madrid School for painting, sculpture and
engraving, June 14th, 1926" • • •

At the Beaux-Arts in
Madrid, the nude portrait
room, around 1922.
Bottom left, Dali, the
school's *enfant terrible*.

A highly unacademic apprenticeship

Archives of the Royal Beaux-Arts Academy of Madrid confirm the passing of a young Salvador Dali through this venerable institution from 1922 to 1926. But in these four student years, he was clearly far more noted for his singular rebelliousness of spirit than for any pictorial genius.

Painting relentlessly, landing his first exhibitions and becoming friends with Lorca and Buñuel, Dali shows only a highly relative, essentially selective, interest for the various subjects taught.

In his second year, when the director announces the appointment of a new teacher whom Salvador considers inept for the job, he leaves the room. This leads to his expulsion from the Academy for a year. And the matter does not stop there. Fellow students use this as a pretext for a politically orientated demonstration for which Dali, rapidly designated as the instigator, is condemned and sentenced to thirty-five days in prison.

After a quick recovery from his detention which he qualifies as "a good opportunity to think and work," he reintegrates the Academy a year later. In 1929, just after a first trip to Paris and a meeting with Picasso, the time has come for final exams. When asked to select a single topic from three randomly chosen ones, he questions the fundamental competence of his examiners, before pulling out of his own free will. This time he has gone too far, and he is definitively expelled from the Academy.

EXPOSICIÓ
S. DALÍ

GALERIES DALMAU
BARCELONA

Dali's first exhibition at the Dalmau Gallery in Barcelona in 1925, where he is noticed by Miró.

Salvador Dali, student, is given a most surprising final report:

Ancient Art History: Pass with honors.
Anatomy / Statue drawing / Pose drawing: Pass with merit.
Relief / Color and composition / Drawing in movement: Refused.
Study of architectonic form / Scientific drawing: Absent.
History of Modern and Contemporary Art: Expelled by decision of the disciplinary advisory committee.

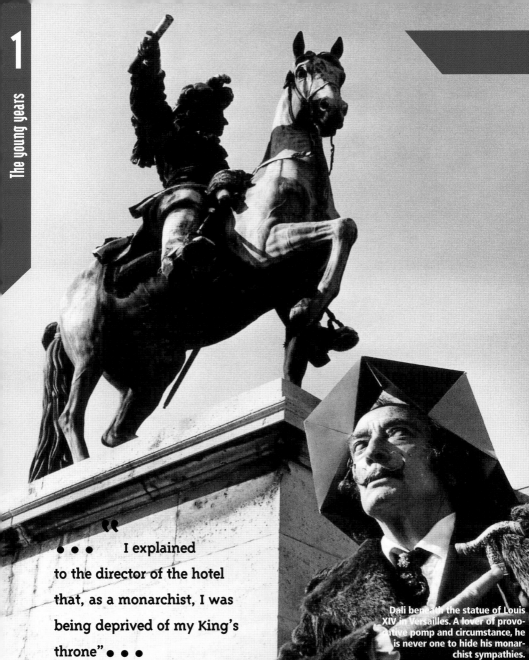

" • • • I explained to the director of the hotel that, as a monarchist, I was being deprived of my King's throne" • • •

Dali beneath the statue of Louis XIV in Versailles. A lover of provocative pomp and circumstance, he is never one to hide his monarchist sympathies.

The throne of my King

When Dali likes to say he is a monarchist, he is no doubt being totally sincere in this respect. His first meeting with the King dates from 1922, when Alphonse XIII makes an official visit to the Royal Beaux-Arts Academy in Madrid, where the eighteen-year-old Catalan is a student.

This visit is somewhat of a farce since the monarch is highly contested at the time. Moreover, the school, practically insalubrious, has very few students enrolled. To mask this situation, the director rounds up all the troops, evidently forbidding them even the slightest misdemeanor or mark of disrespect, and has them clean the school from top to bottom.

But the height of the subterfuge is that students are obliged to bolt from room to room through interior staircases to give the King the impression that the school is teeming with budding artists. Always the same few, seen sometimes facing, sometimes from behind …

In any case, this burlesque visit fires the imagination of Dali whose admiration for the monarch is to reach near fetishist proportions many years later. It is not by sheer coincidence that the Master installs, year after year, his Parisian headquarters in the "Alphonse XIII" suite of the Hotel Meurice.

Alphonse XIII (1886-1931), King of Spain, who made a memorable visit to the Beaux-Arts in Madrid.

When Dali notices that the suite's old wooden toilet seat has been replaced by a new plastic one, he scandalizes the palatial hotel by protesting until the discarded seat is finally found in the junk. Having verified to his satisfaction that the inscriptions engraved on it are authentic, the Master then retrieves the object for his home in Port Lligat.

And why all this uproar? "I want this seat because it has been garnished with, and had the honor to feel, the balls of Alphonse XIII," Dali retorts.

Gala and Dali: a love affair at first sight, to last for over half a century.

"● ● ● For years I lived on false childish theories, crazy fears and anguish of which Gala cured me. Without her, I would have gone mad" ● ● ●

Gala conquers Dali

Elena Diakonoff is her real name. Russian, born in Kazan at a date that biographers place somewhere between 1890 and 1896 (she never having elucidated the matter herself), the future Gala Dali, an atypical personality with a rare destiny, identifies from the start with the man whose life she will share for fifty-three years …

On her arrival in Switzerland shortly after the Great War, she crosses paths with a certain Eugène Grindel, later to become a famous poet under the pseudonym of Paul Eluard. He is the one to first call her Gala, a name she definitively adopts. They marry soon after and have a daughter, Cécile.

But in 1923, the couple embark on an adventure both unusual and audacious for the time: the *ménage à trois*. An infernal trio composed of a Paul Eluard, flighty and consenting, the young surrealist painter Max Ernst and a Gala, vacillating between husband and lover and adored by both. This combination, a source of much amusement to surrealists of the time, lasts until the wife of Max Ernst puts her foot down.

The poet Paul Eluard (1895-1952), Gala's first husband.

It is therefore a vague, fragile couple who, with their eleven-year-old daughter and friends (including the Magrittes), come to visit the young Salvador Dali in Cadaquès in the summer of 1929. Rumor has been spreading about this Catalan artist. They are curious to learn more about his art and certain tendencies, notably scatological ones which, clearly evident in a recent painting, they find disconcerting.

Whatever actually happens that August, the eccentricities of the young Salvador are apparently not displeasing to Gala who, sounding the mysteries of his personality, attaches herself a little more each day. At the end of the holiday, husband, daughter and friends return unaccompanied, leaving behind them a newly formed couple, a Dali, gone from bordering on hysteria to being madly in love, and a Gala, more solid than ever, whispering to her new lover and future husband: "My little one, we shall never leave each other now …"

"... The only thing the world can never get enough of, is exaggeration" ...

A few members of the surrealist group in 1930. From left to right: André Breton, Salvador Dali, René Crevel and Paul Eluard.

A surrealist eviction

On Monday the 5ᵗʰ of February, 1934, Dali is expected at André Breton's home, 42, rue Fontaine, the seat of the surrealist movement. The order of the day, received by all the members of the movement, is: "Dali having been found guilty on several counts of counter-revolutionary acts extolling Nazi fascism, the undersigned propose to exclude this fascist element from surrealism and oppose it by all the means at their disposal."

Having joined the movement five years before, the eccentric Dali has been meaning to break for a long time with the "Pope" of surrealism and his cardinals. He will be the first of many to do so. His description of Hitler as "a terribly fantastic, fascinating surrealist phenomenon," indeed a "perfectly edible" one, is the last straw, leaving no doubt about the outcome.

In the surrealist camp, Aragon, a confirmed communist, is totally unable to accept such conduct and becomes Dali's most virulent opponent. Breton himself has a great admiration for the Catalan and his parano-critical method. Finding himself obliged to take a stand in this matter, or run the risk of losing his leadership altogether, he acts without great conviction.

Belonging to a movement, as surrealist as it may be, goes against the grain of Dali's provocative, independent spirit. Moreover, provocation beyond taboo having become second nature to him, he considers the dozen members of the movement to be of lukewarm, middle-class descent: "The difference between the surrealists and myself, is that I <u>am</u> a surrealist," he was to amuse himself by saying much later.

But the tribunal that lies in wait for Dali that day is to witness one of the most incredibly surrealist masquerades imaginable. The Master arrives feverish with a thermometer in his mouth. Wearing six or seven thick sweaters, he begins to take them off as accusations rain upon him, declaiming poems of Lautréamont, losing his socks and finally throwing himself at the feet of Breton, the inquisitor, with the words: "Every night I dream of fucking your ass," to which the pope of surrealism phlegmatically replies: "I wouldn't recommend it!"

André Breton (1896-1966) the intransigent leader of the surrealists who opts for the excommunication of Dali.

"• • • My father's pain would be rewarded a hundred times over to see me as famous as this"**• • •**

Dali's father (86 years old) and sister Ana Maria in 1949 with Salvador, recently returned from the States. Father and son were reconciled in 1940.

Paterfamilias

Salvador Dali y Cusi, father of the Divine Dali, is the notary in Figueres, and therefore somewhat in the public eye. Despite being fairly broadminded, even calling himself an anarchist, he still has a certain standing to uphold in the Catalonia of the turn of the century. His firebrand son is cause for great distress …

If his father agrees to Dali's studying art, he expects to see him become a teacher, not a painter, and certainly not a painter expelled in scandal from the Academy. But when Dali joins the surrealist movement, his father's vexation is far greater. Now he sees his son as just a clown.

Dali and his sister Ana Maria in Cadaquès in 1926.

However, when his son and heir exhibits a painting in Paris on which he has written: "Sometimes I enjoy spitting on the portrait of my mother," this is the last straw. Salvador's mother has been dead for eight years, and his father has remarried her sister, making these words ambiguous. They are perhaps not aimed at the woman one thinks.

In any case, Dali's father, already very suspicious of Gala, an "adventuress," a married woman, older than his son, and Russian to boot, will have nothing more to do with him. Salvador, realizing that this time he has maybe overstepped the mark, tries to have Ana Maria, his beloved sister, and Raphaël, his benevolent uncle, mediate for a reconciliation with the paterfamilias … but the reply is a blank refusal.

The reunion occurs only after nineteen years, on Salvador and Gala's return from their exile in America. His father final words having been: " you will end up as a penniless louse," the couple take great pains to refute his bleak prediction by rolling into Cadaquès in a gigantic black Cadillac with Gala draped in a mink coat, in the middle of July!

...**P**ainting, sculpture, literature, cinema, the stage ... No creative field holds any secret for the Divine Dali. A transcendent artist, his intense creativity leaves a trace of his genius wherever he goes...

2 The creative artist

"

• • •   Botched or not, paintings integrate and
arrange, to the greatest possible degree, the reflections of
my knowledge and my sensibility" • • •

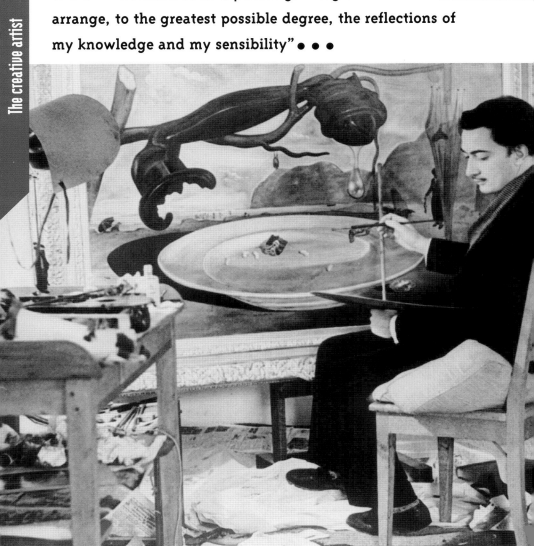

**Salvador Dali painting for his next exhibitions
in the thirties. He is beginning to become famous.**

A conscientious painter

The one area where Salvador Dali never calls a bluff, and is never futile or illusory, is in his work as a painter. In the peace and quiet of Port Lligat and the intimacy of his atelier, where only Gala has the right to disturb him, and where she often reads to him, is produced the one thing he never feigns, his work.

Up at dawn, he goes straight to the easel. Before beginning work, he can stay for several days meditating in front of the white canvas, without touching a single pencil or brush, ordering the slightest details of the subject and the composition in his mind. Normally hyperactive, at such times he is infinitely patient, taking sometimes several months to add the finishing touches to major works.

For *The train station in Perpignan* for example, he finishes the little wooden shoe in the center with a microscopic one-or two-haired brush for hours on end, in order to highlight the slightest contours, shadows and transparencies. For him, mystery has to derive from absolute correctness for his vision to be successfully communicated.

As with every artist, each completed work, despite giving way to another and going off to live its own life, still remains dear to his heart. He is very concerned by a call from the National Gallery in Washington to say that in his famous painting *The Last Supper*, acquired ten years earlier, the yellow in the center has begun to change color. At least that is the impression of the museum curators.

He immediately goes to Washington with his secretary but, as it turns out, today the museum is closed. When he explains who he is, the guards consent to let him in, but only with an escort of five or six museum staff. Unable to see anything from where he stands, he puts his glasses on the tip of his nose and nimbly hops over the barrier before the painting to take a closer look.

At which point he and his secretary are immediately seized, carted off and thrown out by guards who, already suspicious of the strange guy with the moustache, lose no haste in classifying the conscientious painter as a vandalizing delinquent.

Painting at the zoo in Vincennes.

“ ... The Master thinks my film is a flop, though he does agree that <u>he</u> can be seen to function in it unlike anyone else. The shooting was a continual struggle, but fighting with Dali is far better than with an imbecile” (Jean-Christophe Averty) • • •

Dali works with the very best. Above, his set design for Alfred Hitchcock's *Spellbound* with Gregory Peck and Ingrid Bergman (1945).

Dali on screen

At a young age, the Master is interested in cinema as a medium for surrealist thought. Collaborating closely with his friend Buñuel on the production of *Un Chien andalou* in 1929, already a true reflection of Dali's major preoccupations, he re-offends the following year with *L'Age d'Or*. These two important films are his ticket into the surrealist circle.

Despite the controversial success of these two productions, Dali is quick to abandon the cinema. Unable to bear the collective nature of this mode of expression, he wants to make movies where he can direct each stage himself, a practically impossible task. "The photographer is an idiot, and so is the director. And of course, the end result is just the work of a dozen idiots!" he often repeats.

In 1945, he collaborates with Hitchcock on the famous dream sequence of *Spellbound*, then on a project, subsequently aborted, with the Marx Brothers, and on the beginning of an animated film for Disney, *Destino*, of which only eight seconds are shot before the project is abandoned.

He has two more attempts, a first time with his friend Descharnes for *The Lace-maker of Vermeer* in 1954 and a second time in 1966 for *A Soft Self-portrait*, a hilarious creation of the stormy partnership between Averty and Dali, released in America (where Dali's voice is dubbed by Orson Welles) but censored for six years in France.

In fact, the cinema does not really smile on the Divine Dali, and the feeling is mutual: "Painting is the pure work of art, because painting goes in through the painter's eye and out through his hands. There are no intermediaries. And if it's shit, at least it's your own shit!"

Dali and Gala with the Disney couple. Dali and Disney worked together on *Destino*, an ambitious surrealist animation project which never saw the light of day.

"

● ● ●   The number of perceptible images is limited only by the degree of paranoia already in the mind of the spectator" ● ● ●

The invisible man,
Dali, 1929-1933.

Behind the mirror

Salvador Dali was always clear about being an artful master in lying and dissimulation, not only in what he said and wrote, but also in his painting. Despite all the exhibitions, attention and critical studies devoted to his Art, the Master is adamant: "Up until now, only an infinitesimal part of the representations composed into my work has been perceived."

From the beginning of the 1930s, Dali strives, like Arcimboldo and Delacroix before him, to work on the idea of the double or triple image in his painting. But unlike his predecessors who were to only occasionally employ this technique as a stylistic exercise, he develops it, and in time, perfects and complicates it.

First to appear are *The Invisible Man and Woman transforming herself into a Horse or a Lion* where the Master proposes two or three images in one. This then becomes more complicated in very elaborate works like

Slave Market with the disappearing bust of Voltaire, **1940. Dali saw in this painting the image of Gala's love (on the right) annihilating skepticism.**

Apparition of face and fruit-dish on a beach or *Enigma without end* in which a keen eye can distinguish up to five or six images and numerous suggestions. In his watercolors, drawings and prints, he often dissimulates the outline of a mouth, a foot, a hand or even a sexual organ into his work. He either transforms them, giving them totally new and unpredictable meanings, or shrouds them as beneath a veil in the hope that, semi-transparent, the hidden element will come to haunt the spectator's mind.

These subterfuges can even fool those closest to him and most accustomed to his practices. Thus, a year after the marriage of his secretary, Dali asks the young Moore couple to come to his room at the St. Regis. He blindfolds them, sits them down and shows them a magnificent gouache on an easel representing a couched woman, a work dedicated to them. The couple go into raptures, thanking him for this belated gift and step back to contemplate the work. But about three yards away, this young woman is seen to evaporate into a portrait of General Franco.

• • • **A**mong his other (numerous) particularities, Dali never had a "regular" art dealer • • •

"How I paint" …
Dali has an inexhaustible creativity that he applies to the most varied art forms.

An artist without a dealer

Most great painters have an agent or a gallery behind them defending their interests throughout their career. Dali's name can be affiliated to no-one. The couple Gala – Dali handle the promotion of his works themselves, and do so not too badly at all.

The case of Dali is undeniably quite special. He begins to paint at a very young age and reaches his artistic maturity around 1930. At only twenty-six, he has already written the scenario of Luis Buñuel's *Un Chien andalou*, exhibited in Barcelona, collaborated with Lorca, and met Gala.

Quick to be spotted by Picasso, Miró and the surrealists, the sparks are already flying and even if the public at large still ignore the work and the personage, certain connoisseurs make no mistake.

A relentless worker, his oil paintings, works on paper, illustrations, stage-settings, scenarios, writings, exhibitions, happenings, lectures, globe-trotting, along with all sorts of collaborations, follow in rapid succession. He is a veri-

Gala played the role of artistic agent for Dali and took great care of his interests.

table hive of creative activity. This is why the number of his painted works is, in fact, relatively modest compared to that of his contemporaries. Additionally, he will often devote a great deal of time to working on an important painting.

Each painting, on completion, quickly finds a buyer. The first go to aristocratic or collector friends (de Noailles, Faucigny-Lucinge, Julien Green …). Sir Edward James, an English patron, is followed by the American couple, Eleanor and Reynolds Morse, and then by museums, art-lovers and various contacts throughout the world.

The Dali couple never take market value into consideration. They do it on a day to day basis, with no cash flow and no private stock of paintings. When an important retrospective exhibition is organized, or later when the Dali Museum in Figueres is created, this lack of works in the artist's atelier actually proves to be a source of great difficulty. For the Master is then obliged to ask for works back which are already sold, a rather extraordinary thing to do.

• • • The Master's signature: maybe not the easiest way to identify his work • • •

In the salons of the Hôtel Meurice, Dali signing in the company of Pierre Argillet (seated on the left) and Captain Moore (standing). In the mirror, the singular reflection of a camel …

Signing the works

On finishing a work, an artist carefully adds his signature, a personal hallmark which, among other attributes, can play a role in determining the authenticity of the work. A signature has certain characteristics: the writing itself, its movement, direction, size and position. But in this too, Dali differs from his contemporaries by signing, from his initial works, in infinitely different ways.

The complete and relatively precise "Salvador Dali" added to his early works, becomes occasionally, after his meeting with his muse and companion in 1929, a "Gala Salvador Dali." This is further complicated after the war by the adoption of a "Dali" monogram with two legible consonants and two vowels often fantastic and very erratic. However, most of the paintings and drawings being well-known and catalogued, specialists do manage to sort out the wheat from the chaff.

For editions of prints, when the editor brings Dali one or two hundred examples to sign, it's a veritable ceremonial, and nightmarish to manage. The Master hates signing in bulk, admittedly a rather fastidious task. It is advisable to bring, along with the proofs themselves, a ton of pencils, for Dali breaks one every two minutes. It is also advisable to whisk the autographed pages away as quick as lightning, keeping one's eye on him all the time.

For when Monsieur Dali signs, he also does interviews, sings at the top of his lungs, dictates telegrams and holds telephone conversations. That's when signatures take on the color of the conversation and are liberally adorned with crosses, umbrellas, or snails, which can afterwards be disorientating to some.

Dali signing, sometimes painstakingly, sometimes in an offhanded way.

Ironically, when the market is swamped in the 1970s and 1980s with thousands of fakes of 20th century masters, Dali included, counterfeiters have a tough job hiding behind this multitude of signatures. By signing "Dali" always in the same way, they even botch their forgeries so completely that nowadays specialists are even able to declare: "a fake Dali signed by …"

"••• In the 20th century, I am about to revive techniques forgotten since the 21th. In anticipation of the future holograph, I am using a technique of stereoscopic photography" • • •

1975, Dali working on *Gala looking at the Mediterranean Sea which twenty meters away transforms itself into a portrait of Abraham Lincoln*, in his atelier at the St. Regis Hotel in New York.

Three dimensional works

Salvador Dali is the perfect subject for a photographer and most certainly one of the most immortalized 20th century personalities in this respect. A lesser known fact is that the Master has been using photography as a basis for his work from the outset and even takes on certain big names in the field from time to time as creative auxiliaries.

His studio is always littered with photographs and post-cards. Though he faultlessly reconstructs the bay of Port Lligat and the rocks of Cape Creus from memory for a painting done in New York, for any other object, personage or place composed into a work, he needs a concrete visual reference.

In the 1940s, he meets in New York the photographer Philippe Halsman who, for many years, would take magnificent portraits of Dali. Their complicity is total. Whenever Halsman needs an idea for an original shot, he calls the painter who gives him one, and inversely, whenever Dali has a crazy idea that he wants to represent, he knows the photographer will be able to help.

From 1970, the Divine wishes to treat the third dimension in his painting and needs the help of a photographer to test the procedure of the double or triple image before applying it in paint. Many flee this daunting task, but Marc Lacroix, a talented French photographer, takes the time to consider the problem. He repairs an old stereoscopic camera and begins shooting in the winter of 1972.

He makes several portraits of Dali and Gala posing in the studio, or in their room, next to a mirror and an easel, creating each time a very beautiful composition with his superb lighting. The Master then faithfully transcribes the photographs onto the canvas, respecting tiny lags that allow the visualization of the work in relief. From this collaboration are born several three dimensional paintings which astound when exhibited in the Parisian retrospective of the artist at the Pompidou Center.

Dali looking at a slide of one of his works.

39

...**D**ali has no fixed gallery and is relatively ignored by cultural institutions. To survive, he often has to fall back on collectors ● ● ●

A couple of aficionados

Occasionally life's chance encounters are amazingly important. In striking up a conversation with Mr. Reynolds Morse in the men's room of the St. Regis Hotel bar in New York in 1943, Dali has no clue that this man is to become his most faithful collector …

Eleanor and Reynolds Morse, newly wed, well-off industrials from Cleveland, Ohio, where they manufacture moulds for plastics, acquire their first Dali painting in New York in 1943. Both are immensely attracted to the persona, his work and his universe, a passion to prove rather quickly a veritable vocation.

Each year, the couple buy several paintings and drawings, follow the artist to Cadaqués, to Paris and almost anywhere for a major exhibition. They learn Spanish, and everything about their idol, buy manuscripts, out of print catalogues and find themselves some twenty-five years later with over a hundred oil paintings, a great number of works on paper and impressive archives.

Then they are faced with the problem of how to conserve such a collection, and how to protect it in the future. So they open the first Dali museum in 1971 in the very same building as their offices and factory in Cleveland. Rightly esteeming themselves the holders of the most important Dali collection in the world, they contact the important American

Eleanor and Reynolds Morse, friends and faithful collectors of Dali.

museums with a view to eventually donating the collection. But to their horror, all refuse! The few institutions vaguely interested consent to keeping at the most four or five paintings and selling all the rest.

After several years of searching and a series of disappointments, the United States Marine Corps grant the Morse couple a plot of land and buildings in Florida. Thus, since 1982, the artist's greatest masterpieces are open to a large public at the "Salvador Dali Foundation", 1000 Third Street, Saint Petersburg, Florida, USA.

One of the most famous paintings in the Morse collection: *The discovery of America by Christopher Columbus* **(1958-59). One of those mythological or historical themes dear to Dali.**

"

●●● I want my reader to learn, with baited breath, as much about the Dali atom as I know already" ●●●

A man of letters

The list of works that Dali published in his lifetime is so impressive, it makes us wonder how, between painting and his public life, he ever found the time to write so much: diaries, prefaces, scenarios, poems, letters, speeches, short stories, lampoons, major works and even a novel.

His wide knowledge of literature, science and philosophy proves him to be an assiduous reader. When an editor, in commissioning illustrations for a literary classic, hands Dali a copy of the text, the latter is often heard to reply: "There's no need, I know this text and this author perfectly." And in the case of Sade, Lautréamont or Sacher Masoch, he knows them by heart.

From the age of fifteen, he keeps a diary, edited in 2000 as *Diary of an adolescent genius*. He later corresponds extensively with Lorca, and then brings out *Surrealism at the service of the revolution*, *The conquest of the irrational*, *The secret life*, *The cuckolds of old modern art* and *The diary of a genius*, to cite only the essential.

Very early on, Dali gets used to putting ideas on paper. The pen is an indispensable complement to his brush. What is harder to determine though, with this king of deceit and hoax, is whether these texts set out to explain his vision of the world, his personality and his work, or to only partly unveil the mystery.

The cuckolds of old modern art. **In this evocatively entitled lampoon, Dali, whose masters are Vermeer and Velázquez, attacks mainly abstract painters.**

The Master's principal writings are generally corrected and adapted by the French writers Michel Déon and Louis Pauwels. But when André Parinaud, in *How to become Dali* takes a few liberties in transcribing Dalinian thought, the Divine reacts, demanding that any of his own words be highlighted in bold in the book. At least then the reader can discern when something is from the horse's mouth, and when it is not.

For Dali, especially known as a painter, writing was an important medium. He published eleven books, including a novel.

" The stupidest phrase in the French language is 'bête comme ses pieds'"

[lit: *as stupid as his feet,* meaning: *as thick as a brick*] ● ● ●

The ballet *Lumière* by Maurice Béjart, premièred in 2001

A message for Béjart

In 1961, Maurice Béjart is preparing the choreography for the *Ballet de Gala* to be premièred at La Fenice in Venice, and then performed at the Théâtre de la Monnaie in Brussels and at the Théâtre des Champs Elysées in Paris. Scenario, sets and costumes are by Salvador Dali, which does not simplify the choreographer's task …

The ideas, pure "dalirium" as is to be expected, are almost impossible to adapt to the limitations of the stage. The Master insists on things like a wall of Harley Davidson motorbikes for the theatre curtain, a large floppy clock, in working order for an actor has to listen to it ticking, a real beef carcass suspended over the stage, and gigantic models of elephants mounted on stilts.

Usually fairly accommodating, Dali seems rather intransigent about this production, threatening legal action if his ideas are not all scrupulously implemented (he does sue later) and Béjart is extremely hard put to reconcile the different demands.

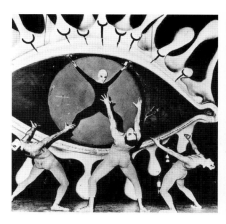

The *danseuse étoile* **Ludmilla Tcherina during a performance of the *Ballet de Gala* at La Fenice in 1961.**

Scheduled to discuss certain details with Dali, the choreographer phones to excuse himself. He has to postpone the appointment. "It's not a problem," answers the Master, "I have an interview tomorrow night for Barcelona television, be watching at 9 p.m." The next day at the set time, Dali tells the interviewer that he has nothing of interest to declare to the public, but a couple of important things to say to Maurice Béjart.

"My dear Béjart, have a good look at this, a miniature replica of what I plan to do on stage in La Fenice." A tub of soapy water appears on the screen into which he dips little wire cubes, permitting the blowing of "the first cubic soap bubbles …" Though Dali's wild imaginings for this project are not all realized, cubic soap-bubbles do blow out of a well during the performances.

Using a live television program to send a message to one person, is just another eccentric factor of this decidedly surrealist ballet.

...Dali's genius lies as much in his mastery of the most elaborate creative techniques as in his capacity to create from next to nothing●●●

The Christ from trash, in Dali's garden in Port Lligat. Sixty feet long, one knee is an old coffee grinder, the other a chamber-pot.

Ex nihilo

One of the most genial aspects of the painter lies in his capacity, on reflection, to assemble and transform insignificant trivia into perfectly coherent, innovative works of art ...

Dali has extravagant ideas like hat-slippers or hat-cutlets, and a sofa in the form of the lips of Mae West. He creates the "ovociped" (an ovoid futuristic means of locomotion), and the harquebus lithograph (a procedure of engraving stone plates by shooting bullets). He also has a rectangular cleft made in the floor of his small studio in order to raise and lower large paintings with a pulley.

In the mid 1950s, when asked to design a night club for Acapulco, he first gives his clients, taken aback, the empty shell of a sea urchin saying: "there's your cabaret." Then he presents them with a drawing and a model where the project can be seen to consist in a monumental sea urchin raised on its spines. The entrance to the club is an elevator through the digestive tube. A totally revolutionary architectural project, not unrealizable, but abandoned for its cost.

A few years later, a big storm throws up all sorts of rubbish on the beach at Port Lligat: tiles, branches, bits of rubber, chamber-pots, electric appliances, the skeletal remains of small fishing boats. Dali, contemplating all this from his window, immediately stops municipal rubbish men from carting everything off to the local dump and asks them to transport the whole lot to the olive grove above his house.

The workers do exactly as he says, no longer surprised by anything to do with the Master, and leave everything dumped in his garden. Like an alchemist and in total secret, Dali goes through the lot and assembles little bits of nothing to make a figure of Christ, sixty feet long, lying on the ground. Very proud of his find, for years he conducts visits of his *Christ with trash*, immortalized by numerous photographers.

In 1959, Dali presenting his "ovociped," a self-designed revolutionary means of transportation. Initial tests were very tough on Dali, here jammed in the cockpit.

47

"... Everything in me is theatrical, I could not have chosen a better place" • • •

The interior of the museum in Figueres is a reflection of Dali himself, surrealistic and grandiose.

Theatre, museum and tomb

From the beginning of the 1970s, perhaps influenced by the Cleveland (Ohio) inauguration of the foundation of Eleanor and Reynolds Morse, his most faithful collectors, Dali starts thinking about a Museum in Spain.

After much discussion, his home town of Figueres offers him the old municipal theatre, a veritable ruin bombed out during the Civil War and burned down by Moroccan vagrants using armchairs for fire-wood. Not much to start with, but Dali's imagination takes care of the rest.

Everyone is called upon to help. Firstly talented architects like Pinero who creates the famous geodesic dome, and then collectors, friends and artists like Fuchs or Pixot who are asked to wrack their brains to find a solution to the lack of major works at Dali's disposal. The Master is busy making frescoes and theatrical decors.

All these efforts finally pay off in 1974 with the inauguration of the Teatre-Museu Dali in which are reinstalled, according to the Master's wishes, the urinals from Maxim's, redecorated for the occasion! The building, meeting all expectations, is unforgettable and incredibly Dalinian. The content, rather poor and mainly theatrical during the first years, subsequently becomes richer, thanks to the systematic buying of major works, made even more possible now by the fact that it is the second most visited museum in Spain after the Prado.

Most of the thousands of visitors contemplating the geodesic dome of the main hall have no idea that they are walking on the tomb of the master builder himself. Maestro Salvador Dali, ultimate eccentric before the Eternal, is in fact the only artist in the world to have been buried in his own museum.

Olé!

The facade of the museum of Figueres. A reminiscence of Port Lligat, the eggs on the roof are still there.

...**O**f a tormented, readily

mystical nature, Dali likes to have

fun more than anything. More or

less innocent, his escapades, treated

as an art, can be extremely daring in

their inventiveness. Even the victims

ask for more • • •

3 The entertainer

"

●●● To switch like this from *The Lace-maker* to the Sunflower, from the Sunflower to the Rhinoceros and from the Rhinoceros to the Cauliflower, you really have to have something up top" ● ● ●

**Dali painting a rhinoceros at
the zoo in Vincennes.**

A cock and bull story

In the mid 1950s, Dali re-conquers Paris after a rather long exile in America by choosing to "coherently" amalgamate elements as apparently unrelated as a Vermeer painting, a sea urchin, cosmic goose-pimples and a rhinoceros, in a prodigious parano-critical demonstration …

Fascinated as a child by a print of Vermeer's *The Lace-maker* in his family home, the Master later makes a copy of this famous work in the Louvre. But in this copy, he can see rhinoceros horns. So he goes to paint a live rhinoceros in the Vincennes zoo.

He then discovers that certain logarithmic curves present in his depiction of the rhinoceros and in an enlargement of his copy of *The Lace-maker*, also appear in sunflowers … and in cauliflower. So logically, in a blow up of the Vermeer painting, we should be able to see a cauliflower, a sunflower and a rhinoceros!

This becomes the object of a highly applauded demonstration-lecture at the Sorbonne in 1955, the underlying meaning of which escapes no-one. Dali is driven to and from the university in a white Rolls-Royce, which his friend Georges Mathieu has taken care to fill with a hundred or so … cauliflower!

The Lace-maker **by Vermeer of Delft (1632-1675). Dali had a profound admiration for this artist.**

Also made at the time is a film called *The prodigious story of the Lace-maker and the rhinoceros*, in which he demonstrates how the "shiver of creation" is present in a drop of water. In falling, it begins to bristle with goose-pimples, losing its purity of form … it is in fact turning into a sea urchin! He then notes how the granular texture of sea urchins is identical to rhinoceros skin … which of course leads him back, in a prodigious conclusion, to *The Lace-maker*. Wow!

❝ **•••** Surpassing the world's most beautiful paintings, with an added bonus of
hitherto unknown nuances of color!" **•••**

A Mongolian landscape.

Expedition to the Outer Imagination

The Master has always kept up with scientific progress. Very well documented, he frequently exchanges views with top scientists, often able to see logic in what the average person would see as pure "dalirium." But when he himself announces revolutionary discoveries, better watch out.

In the early 1970s, Dali storms into the room of his friend Robert Descharnes in New York, excitedly holding out a pen, the kind found in all the rooms of the St. Regis Hotel, an ordinary white ballpoint with a little gold band.

The Master affirms that when the pen is held at a certain angle, you can see the battle of the Thermopyles, in the few traces of urea left by his fingers on the gold band. Pursuing this idea, he explains the phenomenon to a German scientific film-maker who, snatching the bait, proposes to shoot the whole thing with microscopic cameras.

In January 1975 appears *Trip to Outer Mongolia*, a film based entirely on a microscopic analysis of the famous pen, with images for which Dali gleefully provides the commentary.

Except that now the gold band has been transformed not just by an unwashed finger, but by the deliberate application of urine. The battle of the Thermopyles is now not the only thing that can be seen. The images also reveal, or so we are told, a "helicopter view of Outer Mongolia scattered with immense hallucinogenic mushrooms."

The most incredible thing about the microscopic images of this hour-long film, is that one always believes what is being said and sees what one is supposed to be seeing. Delirium and mystification raised to the level of genius, bravo Monsieur Dali!

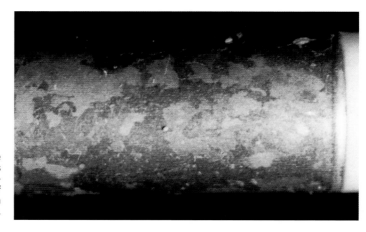

The gold band of the pen from the St.Regis Hotel. Looking attentively, "the Battle of the Thermopyles" can be seen to appear.

55

. . . Dali was not the only organizer of the permanent show he played to the world. He was surrounded by astonishing people **. . .**

Pierre Argillet (left) and Captain Moore around
Dali in the 1970s.

A captain for a secretary

An artist's life, precarious and extravagant, with its indispensable globe-trotting and social events, can never be organized in a traditional way. And the strong personalities of Dali and Gala do not facilitate effective long-term collaboration.

For a long time, Dali's secretarial work is handled by a few close friends or by reception desks in the palace hotels where the couple stay. But they have a great tendency to lose or forget messages. They are in fact, totally disorganized.

John Peter Moore, a former captain of the British secret service, an elegant Irishman with a stunning resemblance to David Niven, becomes the Divine's unofficial secretary in 1964 and is rapidly called "the Captain" by everyone.

Unofficial in the sense that he doesn't have an office, though he always has a room in the same hotel. Business is discussed with complete indiscretion in corridors, hallways, at the bar, in the lobby, or over the general hubbub of the Master's apartment.

Highly intelligent, worldly, refined, good with people, humorous, witty and a speaker of many languages, Moore handles just about anything to facilitate the private life and business of the couple. Working without a fixed salary, he is paid in a more or less fluctuating commission for sales and contracts he has handled, contrary to common practice and despite the sums of money involved.

Ostracized in 1974, he feels the brush off rather deeply and begins to sublimate the idol with whom he no longer is in contact but for whom he still has a profound admiration and a sincere attachment. His collection of the artist's works amassed over the years and housed in one, then two, and finally three museums of Cadaqués, has become a veritable gold mine.

A prince of hoax, a realm where Dali is king, the Captain's eye is ever glued on Dali's property, opposite but a little lower than his own, in Port Lligat, and eventually decides to declare his geographical supremacy for all eternity by prematurely having his own tombstone built just above the house of the Divine.

The future tomb of Captain Moore in the cemetery in Port Lligat, just behind Dali's house.

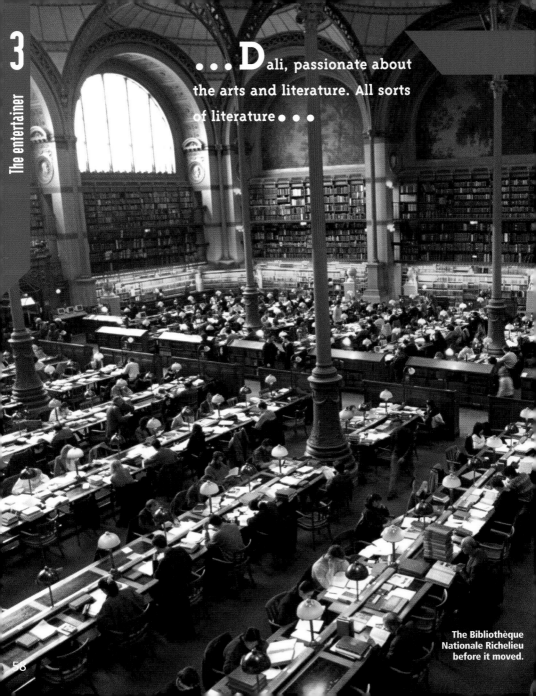

. . . **D**ali, passionate about the arts and literature. All sorts of literature ● ● ●

The Bibliothèque Nationale Richelieu before it moved.

A descent to hell

For many years, the French Bibliothèque Nationale, rue Richelieu, has been planning to have Dali come on an official visit. A date is finally set in 1964 but on the morning the artist is a little tense and thoughtful.

The Master has just had a run in with the press the previous evening when he prematurely leaves a happening, displeased with the way things are going. The morning papers are full of his caprice and the failure of the event, and he is not in an ideal mood for the visit.

Received with due protocol by Mr Adhémar and Mr Héron de Villefosse, directors of the Bibliothèque Nationale, he is ceremoniously shown different works brought out by librarians whom Dali finds to be "spinsters of the Legion of Honor," and then asked to autograph a menu he created thirty years before for a dinner of "Friends of the Marquis de Sade," which he obligingly does.

Suddenly finding this visit a little too official and up-tight, his boyish spirit puts solemnity to flight by asking to be taken to "hell." He wants to see the place where all the erotic works are stored.

When this confidential section is reluctantly opened up, Dali revels in commenting on numerous details of the licentious works, putting his hosts to some considerable embarrassment.

A reinvigorated Dali smirkingly exclaims in leaving: "Serves them right with their gloomy faces when their books are not. I took them to hell!"

Dali and the librarians looking at the famous works …

" ••• For any party, it's good to plan ahead and organize a social salad" •••

Salvador Dali talking with Johnny Hallyday at the Meurice in 1967.

Mornings at the Meurice

The concierge of the Hotel Meurice is always directing visitors to Suite 108 on the first floor, also called the "Alphonse XIII Suite" after another illustrious guest. Receptionists are constantly transferring calls to the same apartment. It is 11 a.m., and according to a well established ritual, Master Dali is holding court.

With practically no screening at all, you often see a greasy hippie just back from Katmandu and a minister in a three-piece suit, both come out of the lift and head for the same door, where they join a heterogeneous group of about thirty people.

Visitors come with something to show, with their fantasies and words of wisdom. "The more confusion, the better …", their host likes to repeat. Over there a Spanish nun chats with a prostitute and two anarchists, here a pretty girl is courted by a loathsome, obese creature. In the Master's entourage: eccentrics, reporters asking questions about everything and anything, editors looking for contracts, hangers-on, the tailor, the telephone …

The sumptuous dining room at the Meurice Hotel in Paris.

In different languages, conversation invokes the dollar, the yen, the peseta, the latest book release, recent exhibitions, the fur fashion shows, the Lido, the Crazy Horse, up and coming Spanish painters … Paco Rabane, Gaudi, Poincaré and John Lennon, all in the same breath.

For dessert: Velasquez, Ingres, Paracelsus, Freud and Saint Theresa of Avila. Some visitors have trouble keeping up with this outrageous intercourse but those who really pay attention usually come out fine. Others leave bedazzled and charmed, but have understood little or nothing at all.

When Gala makes her appearance around 1.30 p.m., the salon empties until the following morning. Dali, refreshing himself with a glass of water, says to his companion: "I had a good time today!" or: "Today, there were only morons!"

"
• • •   My love goes
through my soul, my
eroticism through my
eyes" • • •

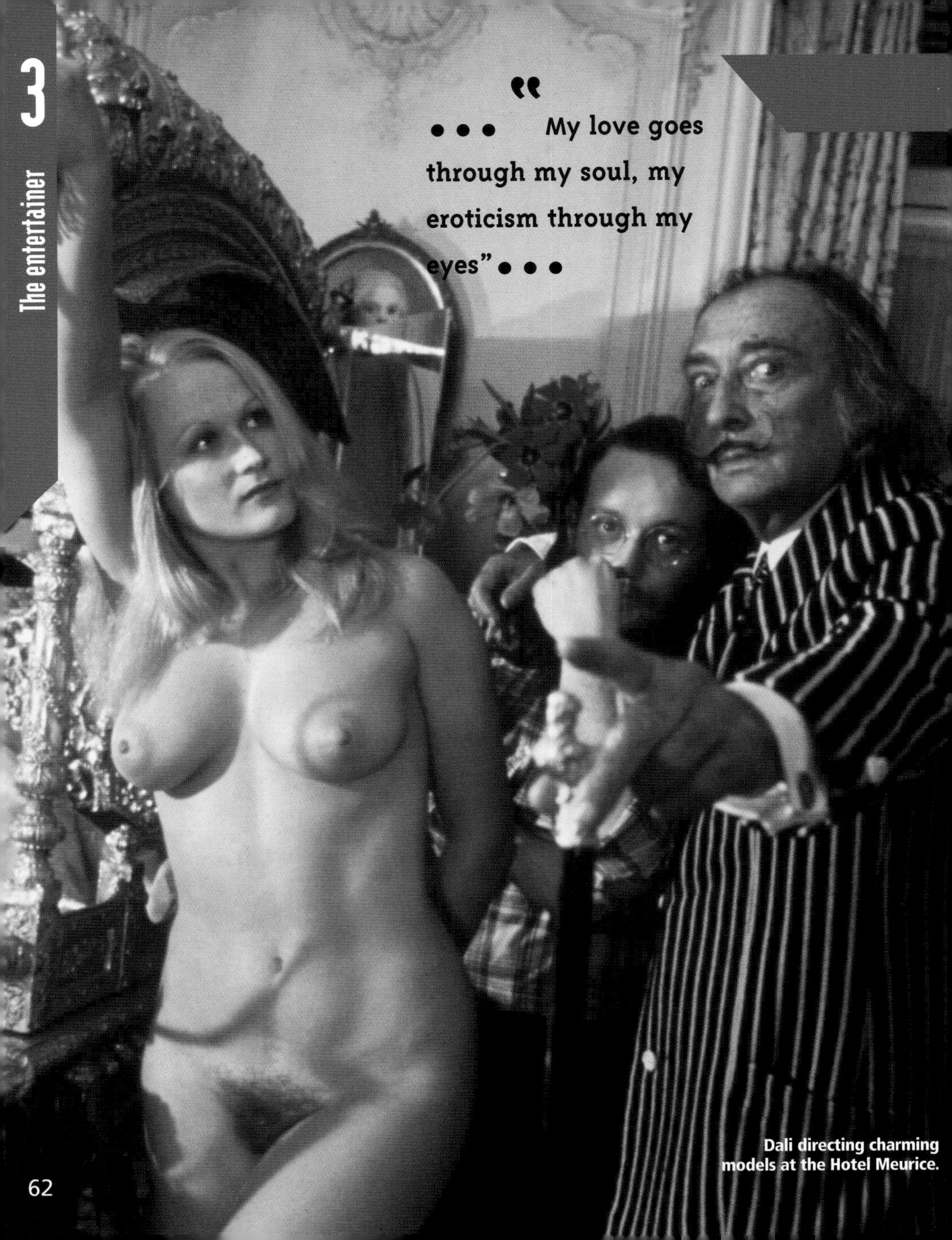

Dali directing charming
models at the Hotel Meurice.

Visual pleasures

Master Dali is an intellectual. Though regularly seen in the company of pretty girls and beautiful, androgynous young men, he never touches them. This he affirms and in truth he does know only one unique woman: Gala. On the other hand, the lady of his heart gives him free rein to organize sessions of a rather peculiar nature in which she never participates.

Dali actually has a "sex officer," a Frenchman with a model agency in Barcelona, who supplies him with "trucks of girls." Dali goes for young women with angelic faces and an ingenuous manner. And boys with solid aesthetic criteria.

A scenario scientifically elaborated in advance by Dali is produced with different actors according to very precise, totally surrealist directions. A clever staging of eroticism, its goal is to arouse in the performers, hitherto unknown to each other, an irreversible desire to continue. At which moment, the Divine intellectual's ultimate pleasure is to revert this desire, turning the sensation into a flop, often to the great annoyance of the participants.

But even the most well prepared scenario can misfire. One day, temporarily appointing Captain Moore, his secretary, as "sex officer," he asks the

The Dream of Venus, **a surrealist representation of the world of the unconsciousness according to Dali.**

latter to take five recently met Gypsy musicians out to a Parisian brothel that night and offer them five girls.

All goes according to plan, except that Dali arrives too late and the Gypsies, highly turned-on, have already finished. The Master, furious, leaves without paying for the caprice, which causes a minor scandal next morning at the reception desk of the Hotel Meurice, when a "madam," aggressive and very vocal, comes to collect her due.

" ● ● ● For Dali, you have to know how to sufferrr" ● ● ●

A Harley Davidson brought to the Hotel Meurice by one of his friends at his request. Dali's demands were always fantastical, and sometimes difficult to satisfy.

"Dali has asked me to ..."

If during all his parties and receptions, Dali wants to get closer to someone he likes, he immediately entrusts him with a mission, launching him on a quest. The person, flattered to have been chosen from all the others, does his very best to satisfy the needs or caprices of the Divine ...

Though their logic and extreme importance is always made clear to the willing candidate, these often fanciful tasks can at times prove difficult if not impossible, costly, and extremely time-consuming.

Thus mandated, the man on a mission, proud as Punch, begins to work like a Trojan, alerting friends and acquaintances with: "Dali has asked me to find him a ..." Occasionally assignments are easy, but more often they are highly extravagant. White clown costumes, Wilhem II's pointed helmet, magic tricks, eccentric bath-tubs, bidets from real brothels, all of which requires devotion and sometimes incredible energy, especially when the task is near impossible.

Dali often avoids losing time having to visit different institutions with this judicious strategy. It also enables him to prepare happenings without spending a cent and keep a low profile at the same time. Any problems, any categorical refusals are faced by the go-between, and Dali's idea has not suffered in the least.

In 1967, to celebrate the loves of Ronsard and Cassandre, Dali mandates an editor to have made a monumental tombstone symbolizing the couple, which must then be placed at the bottom of a Parisian swimming-pool filled with straw instead of water. On the day, Dali arrives to set the pool on fire before an impressive horde of paparazzi. "Not enough straw, I'm out of here!" he exclaims, abandoning a rather perplexed crowd who soon cheer themselves by diving into the refreshments.

Dali liked unusual headgear and gave a lecture in 1961 at the Ecole Polytechnique wearing a Prussian helmet.

"   ●●●   Oh, I feel threatened with a present"
(Dali would often say) ●●●

**Dali playing with
Baboo the ocelot
in Cadaquès.**

Presents, presents

Being admitted into Dali's inner circle, means accepting on occasion to give the Master "suggested presents" he would like to receive. These gifts, always offered elegantly, are a prelude to a long-standing relationship ...

He may choose an object, a whim, a book, or a piece of furniture discovered when strolling with Gala through some quarter of Paris or New York. Perhaps a painting completely overlooked at an antique dealer's, or a pair of stone lions for Gala's mansion in Pubol.

This ritual also works in reverse, for the Master, though he never has a dime in his pocket, is never stingy when it comes to celebrating a happy event, the anniversary of a meeting, a new birth or the marriage of a close friend, by thoughtfully offering a work or a beautiful dedicated drawing.

Captain Moore and his wife in the company of their charming "present."

Though Dali's practical joker side can lead to irritating gifts. Once in New York, while waiting in line with Gala at a movie theatre, he sees an eccentric walking an ocelot, a South American feline between a cat and a tiger. He buys it and has it brought to the St. Regis Hotel, where he asks the concierge to put it in the bed of his secretary, Captain Moore.

When the latter discovers the charming quadruped that night, he immediately sees the painter trying to test his reactions. So the next day he makes no comment, until Dali, unable to bear the suspense any longer, finally asks him: "How do you like pussycat?"

Against all expectations, Captain Moore adopts "pussycat," even gives it a diamond necklace. Baboo becomes yet another pole of attraction around Dali and eventually, a faithful domestic companion to the Moore couple.

3

The entertainer

. . . One of those creatures better to have on the wall than at the table . . .

Dali on the table, in Rome holding his famous glass cane. He was in Italy to illustrate *The Divine Comedy* of Dante.

At the table of the Divine

The couple always like to stay in the same palace hotels when in Paris or New York each year. They also frequent a few famous restaurants, either to invite guests or just have a quiet lunch or dinner together …

When in Catalonia, the couple have few guests and seldom stand on ceremony, opting for the simple gastronomy of Port Lligat. They eat light meals, mainly fish and sea urchins, either on their boat or sitting on the rocks.

But on their way up to Paris, they always stop over in Saulieu or Valence to savor the creations of local master chefs. Usually ordering ortolans (a fowl delicacy), one of their favorite dishes which they eat in style with a towel over their heads to keep the taste.

After the marathon morning receptions at the Meurice, the couple always go out around 2 p.m. for a revitalizing late lunch. During the week they eat at places like Laurent, Lasserre, Ledoyen or Lucas Carton. But on Sundays, they always go to the Tour d'Argent, one of the rare Parisian restaurants open that day.

Invited to a Sunday lunch at friends, Dali seems more attracted to an enormous basket of exotic fruits, all very uncommon at the time, than to the smorgasbord specially prepared for him. He asks his hosts to put one fruit of each variety into a bag, with a little label on each one and its precise name.

He goes straight off to his friend Claude Terrail at the Tour d'Argent asking, when handed the menu, for a specific exotic fruit which, obviously, the restaurant has to excuse itself for not having. Whereupon, he brings it out immediately from under the table, to eat before the astonished personnel and other guests.

Having done this five or six times, Dali finally gets up, takes his cane and leaves with a gruff complaint to a dumbfounded Claude Terrail that his restaurant is really going downhill. Even at the table, Dali likes to have fun.

Dali in the entrance of the Paris restaurant, La Tour d'Argent, where he was a regular but disconcerting client.

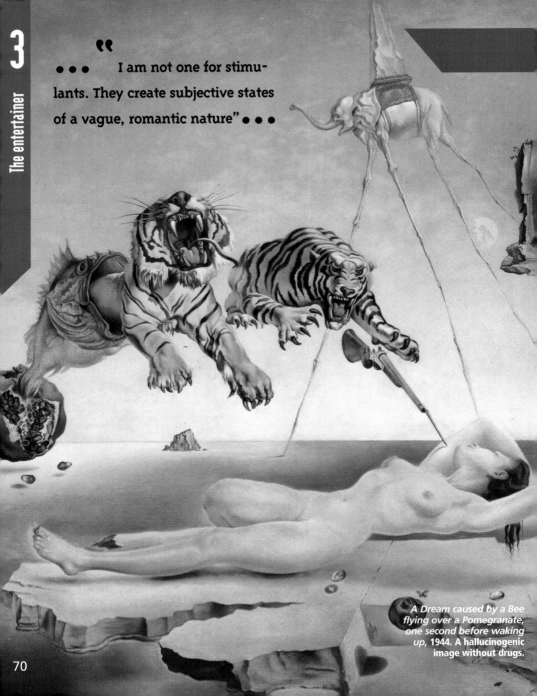

"" ••• I am not one for stimulants. They create subjective states of a vague, romantic nature" •••

A Dream caused by a Bee flying over a Pomegranate, one second before waking up, 1944. A hallucinogenic image without drugs.

Artificial paradises

"The only difference between a madman and me, is that I'm not mad," the Divine Dali repeats incessantly. That may be the case, but how does one explain the wild, fantastical, provocative and so unpredictable character of the public figure? The most plausible explanations seem to be : alcohol, tobacco or other drugs …

❝ No way!", answers the prime suspect when asked this delicate question, "I did smoke and drink a lot at one time, but it was to the detriment of my Art. And faced with a choice between the two, I chose Art." This is also largely confirmed by his intimate friends: the Master needs no added incentive to flirt so blithely with craziness and genius.

About drugs, he is just as adamant, though unlike alcohol and tobacco, he has never touched the stuff. Fascinated by the flower-power movement of the late 60s and often seen in the company of hippies, though he does sometimes publicly vaunt the merits of LSD as a creative stimulant, speaking about it is one thing and taking it another. The day he does try it, he has a rather unfortunate adventure.

In the space of a single evening in November 1967, Dali has to inaugurate the Drugstore Saint-Germain, go to the *Figaro*'s fur show dinner at Lasserre's and, at the invitation of *La Table Ronde*, do a live demonstration of copper engraving before television cameras waiting in the Place des Victoires. With such a seemingly impossible schedule, no-one really expects him to turn up for the last event. But contrary to all expectations, though rather late, Dali turns up in a limousine with a motorcycle escort.

Like a tornado, his cane raised in salute and his eyes hallucinated by what turns out to be LSD, he heads straight for the copper plates, incises them with a few strokes and declares his task accomplished. He leaves as quickly as he came, without giving cameras time to film, nor anyone else a chance to realize what is going on.

The morning after, sober and a little uneasy, he calls the organizers to ask what the engravings look like. When they reply, in all seriousness, that the coppers are exactly in the spirit of two abstract painters he detests, he takes this as a warning and never repeats the experience.

Dali "engraving" coppers in the Place des Victoires.

• • • **A**s provocative in his life as

in his work, Dali was phenomenal

press material. Journalists loved him

for his scandals and his happenings.

Dali's genius also fed his own

image • • •

4 Provocative and popularized

" • • • Escaping out that hole spiked with the stalactites and stalagmites of my anger, seemed the wisest thing to do" • • •

On March 17th, 1939, Salvador Dali leaving the police station with a charge for "disorderly conduct".

A terrific publicity coup

In February 1939, Dali goes to New York for an exhibition at the Julien Levy Gallery, scheduled to begin on March 21ˢᵗ. On his arrival, the department store Bonwitt Teller commissions him to dress two windows for their Spring season. He gets down to work straightaway …

He decides to do them on the theme of Night and Day, installing his creations by dark, after hours. Day is represented by a female wax dummy in a green evening dress staring at a bathtub filled with fur, and Night by a figure lying on a black-covered bed, beneath which fake cinders are seen to glow.

On the morning of March 16ᵗʰ, the store management, having slipped a few "spies" in amongst passing shoppers to test their reactions to the creations, decides to replace the

5ᵗʰ Avenue, New York. The shop window of the Bonwitt Teller department store after Dali's fall.

rather faded dummy of the Day window with a brand new one. Dali, happening to pass by that very afternoon, is livid at the substitution.

He hurls abuse at the management, demanding immediate restitution, and when ignored, rushes like a raging bull into the window in question and starts trying to move the bathtub. Only to lose his balance. And instead of the bathtub, it's Dali himself that falls out through the window, a little nonplussed to find himself on the pavement of 5ᵗʰ Avenue mid all this broken glass!

Barely over the shock, he is arrested by two police officers who have just witnessed everything, and put in jail. The store is suing for "willful damage to the property of others with harmful intent." But the court only upholds a charge of "disorderly conduct" and a few hours later, he is released.

The inconvenience of this night of custody is quickly forgotten when the morning press focuses more on the incident itself, and on this "rather strange young artist." Publicity … which, just four days before an opening, falls with perfect timing.

"... You will end up being a penniless louse" (the famous phrase of Dali's father in repudiating his son and Gala in 1929)...

Avida Dollars

André Breton, who still bears a grudge against Dali, coins this brilliant anagram when the couple leave Europe for America in 1940. A departure not at all prompted (as the pope of surrealism tries to imply), by a love of money, but because Gala is Jewish and the surrealists are persona non grata in Spain …

Far from taking offence and replying to Breton, Dali decides to adopt "Avida Dollars" and exploit it (so he thinks) to his profit, allowing himself even to be provocative on this theme. From this is born the character of the mercenary Dali feeding thirty years of gossip columns with endless declarations about: "the magic of gold, wads of dollars, checks rolling in, dreams about money, etc …"

Those close to him do not see this personage at all. In Cadaqués, Dali appears each day in shorts and an open shirt, sometimes shaven, sometimes not, wearing espadrilles bought for a few pesetas in the village: a long cry from the jabot shirts, velvets and minks that he likes to flaunt in Paris or New York. And even in these two cities, he never knows the value of the money, often astonished at the overjoyed look of a taxi-driver whom he has just tipped with a one hundred dollar bill.

Gala handles the business side, negotiating all his contracts. She holds the strings of the purse with an iron fist, which leads some to say that "Avida Dollars" is more applicable to her than to Dali. Usually so liberal in distributing autographs, he tells all his bankers that a power of attorney signed in favor of his wife will be the only other signature they will ever get from him. Money, in fact, holds practically no interest for him, and sometimes in private he acknowledges that he "needs to earn enough for Gala to pay the bills."

At the death of André Breton in 1966, Dali is amused to read in the poet's death notice a printing of: "J'ai cherché l'or du temps" (I looked for the gold of time). "Strange," says he, "coming from a man who accused me of so much avidity and lumbered me with that famous anagram. Maybe he did look for the gold of time, but me, I found it!"

An American one dollar bill.
Left: Dali disguised as a dollar.

"•••   Picasso is a Spaniard, me too, Picasso is a genius, me too, Picasso is a communist, me never!" •••

The burning giraffe, a **Dali engraving from the** *Bullfight* **series, 1966.**

Pablo Picasso (1881-1973).

78

Picasso-Dali

On any occasion, Dali expresses his most sincere admiration for his older colleague. But an absurd misunderstanding and divergent political views separate them for a long time. In 1965, Dali feels such veneration and has such a strong desire for reconciliation that he decides to photograph the famous Bullfight series of Picasso and re-transcribe it in drypoint, to "dalinise" it …

Completely satisfied with his surrealist version, so reworked that it takes a while to realize that it is based on Picasso, Dali wants to tell the Master of Mougins about it and renew contact with him at the same time. But there seems to be a problem, his telegrams go unanswered. When he manages to get Picasso's number, he calls relentlessly, but a polite secretary replies with tireless repetition that he is not at home.

A telegram from Dali to Picasso announcing that he will be giving a lecture in his honor a few days later.

In the spring of that year Françoise Gilot's book *Vivre avec Picasso* (*Living with Picasso*) is released, in which Picasso is highly criticized. Dali is scandalized, saying that "genius is not to be contested." On May 1st he decides to put several bouquets of lily-of-the-valley beneath a painting of Picasso exhibited in a show at the Grand Palais. Despite the repercussions of this homage in the press, the silence continues.

In the last days of his life, Picasso confides to two very dear friends: "Deep down, I had a great affection for Dali. I would have seen him again with pleasure, he always amused me, but I didn't want him to use our reunion for publicity."

What insurmountable drama could have separated these two artistic geniuses? One day in 1933, Picasso, who believes in Dali, loans him the money for a ticket to New York where he can make contacts. A little carried away by his mounting fame, the Catalan teasingly remarks to friends that now Picasso will be wanting his money back. But he has not bargained with Spanish pride. Piqued, the Master of Mougins says nothing, and closes his door for ever.

... **D**ali was often accused of being a trickster and a poser. He never really pretended to be otherwise ● ● ●

Dali being photographed by a group of young girls in 1960.

Salvador manufactures Dali

Not only do their personalities change, the Dali couple also dress very differently in private and in public …

In Cadaqués, Gala will invariably be in a blouse and jeans or cotton pants, and her famous husband in a kimono, shorts or espadrilles. But in New York and Paris, they always dress with the utmost elegance: Gala in a Chanel suit, with a dark mink in cold weather, always the same one, and Dali in a double-breasted suit, pin-striped or not. Only at certain happenings does the Master wear eccentric clown outfits or underwater diving gear.

But Dali adds his own unique, and immediately identifiable touch to the couple's elegance.

His illustrious moustache is grown at the age of twenty-eight. Originally as fine and horizontal as two pencil strokes, it is only while in the States during the war, that he lets it become fatter and curve upwards. The secret of these "cosmic antennae?" A scrupulous daily waxing with Hungarian balm.

They give him a penetrating look, perhaps equaled only by Picasso. Add a collection of short canes with chiseled silver knobs, brandished on each public occasion, and a speaking voice accentuated by exaggeratedly long syllables, and you get the 20th century painter with the most public appeal.

Dali and Gala beneath an imaginary street sign, the "Rue Salvador Dali."

But sometimes this charismatic personality, able to freeze the noisiest crowds to attention, is put to the test. One evening, on his way back to the hotel, a professional photographer stops him and asks for a picture. With a gesture now become second nature to him, he fixes the camera, staring wide-eyed, and brandishes his cane.

The surprise comes when the photographer gives him a ticket to go pick up his souvenir in a shop around the corner! He rips it up in rage, wondering if anyone else on the planet doesn't know the Divine Dali.

" ••• Sometimes the Divine Dali gets away with things that an ordinary Dali would never be able to" • • •

The Great Masturbator, **Dali, 1929.**

The great masturbator

Giving this title in 1929 to one of his first large-sized paintings already constitutes an act of high surrealism. At the time, his explicit writings and interviews on a practice hitherto only whispered in the secret of confessionals, are either symptomatic of addiction or pure provocation.

Salvador Dali is totally shameless about his practice of onanism, giving detailed revelations of all its subtleties. Not only does he surrender to it totally, a relatively banal fact after all, but he puts it on the same level as his libido or his paranoia as a creative, promotional and inspirational element.

His onanism is however not only mental. Master Dali proves to be, luckily on rare occasions, uncommonly active in the field. In the mid 1940s, while in Hollywood for different projects, he organizes a nude session with Constance Webb, a young model who years later talks about her misadventure.

As she lies relaxing for a moment on the sofa after holding the same pose for a long while, Dali suddenly pounces on her, ejaculates hastily on her breasts and, to top it all off, begins to lick his own sperm. In terror, the young woman flees to the bathroom to wash herself and dress.

She who never in her most erotic dreams could have imagined a tenth of what she has just gone through in a few seconds, returns to find a very debonair Salvador Dali, perfectly at ease, who most respectfully opens the door for her, confiding by way of a passing farewell: "I did not penetrate you because I am faithful to Gala."

Dali paints a nude of Marianne Hoffmann in 1969.

" ● ● ● Dali is becoming more and more Stalinian. What's more, it happens automatically with me: as soon as anyone is insulted or crushed down, I raise him up" ● ● ●

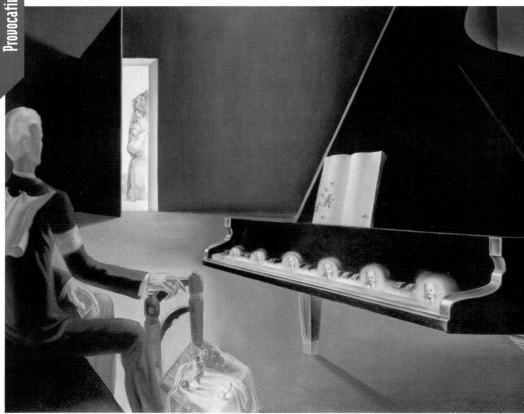

Partial hallucination, Six apparitions of Lenin on a piano, **Dali, 1931.**

The knight of lost causes

A great many Dalinian challenges are provoked by an impetuous need to fight for hopeless causes. Apart from stirring up media attention, disgrace and passionate reaction, they allow him to test to the full his powers of "persuasion"…

From a young age he draws every touchy subject out into the open. The year 1929 is memorable in this respect. April sees the release of *Un chien andalou*, the film produced with Luis Buñuel, with its unforgettable scene of the cutter sectioning the eye. In August Gala, married and the mother of a child, leaves Eluard for him and, in December, during an exhibition in Paris, the young agitator inscribes under a chromolithograph of Sacré-Cœur: "Sometimes I enjoy spitting on the portrait of my mother." A scandalizing attack on both the family and public morals.

Then come his great declarations about scatological leanings, the "edibility" of Hitler, the defense of Stalin, a few phrases in support of Franco, the rehabilitation of the ancient painters, the cuckolds of modern art and the immoderate love declared for gold and silver, at a time when it is thought proper to carefully avoid these delicate subjects.

From then on, public opinion splits irreparably into two distinct camps. Those who take things literally and denounce: "Dali the fascist, Dali the pervert, Dali the villain." And those unconditional supporters who, knowing what to think about all this, simply cry: "This Dali, what a nerve! How will he get out of this one? What will he think of next?"

In 1969, a lady collecting signatures for the abolition of the death penalty creates a scene in Dali's salon at the Meurice. The Master, seeing this, approaches and declares: "As a Catholic, apostolic, and Roman, I am against the death penalty." But as soon as a smile appears on the lady's face, he continues with: "But I am all for torrrture!"

Dali lying on his own bed during the bed-designing competition at the Warwick Hotel on April 26th, 1939, in which celebrities took part. The meaning of the umbrella is not explained. It was an idea of the Master.

" **• • •** When it comes to publicity, others have done a thousand times better than me. Look at Christ, getting yourself nailed to a cross, what propaganda!" **• • •**

Dali posing with himself for a publicity for Lanvin chocolate in 1973, in Paris.

The Dali logo

Salvador Dali's promotional activities are not limited to the famous Lanvin chocolate television advertisement in 1969, or to the images he designs in America during the war for brands of ties and stockings. The product he aims to sell all his life is himself.

Quick to realize that in this new century, talent is not enough for an international career, he tries by all means to come to the forefront of the stage, and stay there in the footlights. He does this unaided, instinctively testing out techniques as good as those employed by professionals in the field.

Going from the simple principle that "being talked about is the most important thing," he deliberately astonishes all the time, pulling every string to attract the press, the cheapest publicity of all.

He composes a public persona, invents defects that he does not have, like avarice, keeps us in doubt about his sanity, transforms his public life into a permanent happening, tells pseudo inside-stories about his onanism, shows off, aggravates and declaims on everything and anything.

His brilliance allows him to always fall on his feet and even if certain arguments he defends are outrageous, the debate takes place and the articles abound, which is exactly what he is looking for. Dali reaps far more benefit from the Lanvin chocolate advertisement than the product itself. And when asked about his reason for doing this publicity, he replies:

"Five minutes devoted to chocolate gives me three years to work on the same painting in a maximum of luxury. Usually people work to earn money. I earn money to be able to work."

Dali in 1961 wearing a Father Christmas costume and a hat of his own design called *The Dali Complex*.

" ● ● ● Instead of saying butterfly, I say bouterreflaaaaiiii" ● ● ●

Dali in 1961 at La Fenice Theater, during a rehearsal of the 18th century comic opera, *Scipio in Spain*. The artist posing in front of his design for this production.

Bouterreflaaaaiiii

Though he speaks perfect French, the language he uses every day, Dali loves to speak English with an atrocious accent, gleefully transforming it into a new, typically Dalinian tongue with well practiced idioms.

These consist in rolling his "r"s as in Spanish, maintaining the thickest of French accents and adding a word of Catalan from time to time. This is a guaranteed success which obliges Anglo-Saxon interviewers to always subtitle the Master's television appearances so that viewers can understand.

Dali remarks that Americans understand practically nothing of what he says, and that when they do miraculously pick up a word or a Dalinian expression, they are euphoric: "As a matter of fact, they are applauding themselves for having understood what I'm saying," he confides.

This little game amuses him enormously and considerably reinforces his original image. In New York, to astound you have to do much more than in Europe. Having fun one day

Steve Allen and Eva Gabor interviewing Dali in front of Saint Patrick's Cathedral, during the 1951 Easter Parade in New York.

zigzagging down the sidewalk of Madison Avenue in a panther fur coat and a Phrygian cap, he remarks to a friend: "Look, it's incredible here, absolutely no-one pays any attention to me!"

In a few cases, his idiomatic expressions become farcical. One night at the St. Regis Hotel, Dali is scared by a strong smell of burning in the apartment. Fearing a fire, he immediately calls his secretary in the next room, who does not answer. Crazy, he rushes out and bangs on a neighboring door, opened by a half-asleep woman in a dressing-gown and hair-curlers.

Completely hysterical, Dali cries "Foc, foc," Catalan for "Fire, fire."

Exasperated by the insane cries of a mustached lunatic in the middle of the night, she slams the door in his face with a: "And fuck you too!"

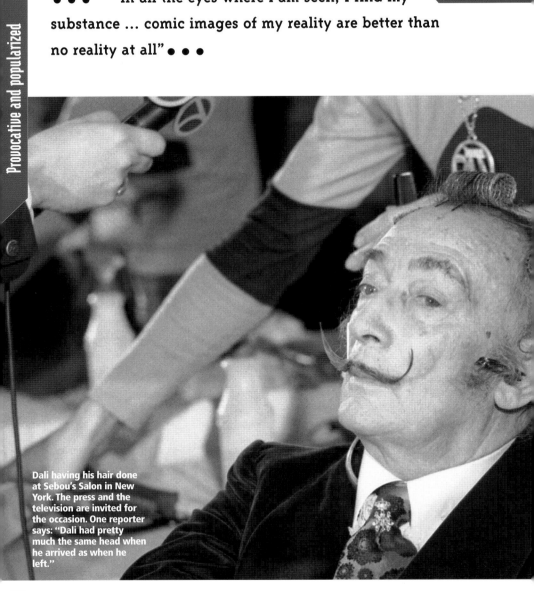

"... In all the eyes where I am seen, I find my substance ... comic images of my reality are better than no reality at all" •••

Dali having his hair done at Sebou's Salon in New York. The press and the television are invited for the occasion. One reporter says: "Dali had pretty much the same head when he arrived as when he left."

The media machine

Dali very quickly grasps the important role the media will play in 20ᵗʰ century society. Not content to remain an obscure, accursed painter, he decides to marry two complementary attitudes: provocation and public outcry.

He has provocation in the blood anyway, no problem there. For the other, he courts and maintains a lifelong relationship with the press. This is his recreation. He understands something very basic. For the cameras to turn, the microphones to be positioned, and the press releases to fly, he has to create an event.

This may consist in incising lithographic stones with bullet shots, signing books dressed as a clown, a cosmonaut, or Father Christmas, bringing a giant twelve meter baguette to a press conference, dressing models as lobsters, lamb chops, coffee spoons … the list is long.

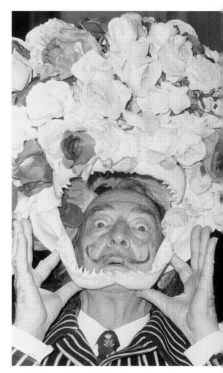

For reporters, Dali, is the ideal "subject." Some never move for anything else, and eagerly await his arrival for the show to begin, in Paris and New York mainly. "The Divine Dali is here" read titles with day by day accounts, hour by hour reports, of a schedule enough to make a politician green with envy.

His planetary fame, on a par with rock stars or heads of state, is quite unique for a painter. And no doubt because, instead of his own paintings, he is selling his escapades and his dalirium.

The deal is very clear. Everyone is happy. Dali gets what he wants. Fame and publicity. And the media gets debate, sensation and controversy. To his detractors, or to friends worried that his real work be

Dali, his head in a shark's jaw decked with roses, in 1975.

completely lost in a lateral drift, he shrugs his shoulders and replies: "Talk about me, talk about me all the time, even if it's only to say good things about me."

"
• • •   I am a very bad painter, but the first
in a period that is worthless" • • •

	Technique	Inspiration	Color	Subject	Genius	Composition	Originality	Mystery	Authenticity
LÉONARD DE VINCI	17	18	15	19	20	18	19	20	20
MEISSONIER	5	0	1	3	0	1	2	17	18
INGRES	15	12	11	15	0	6	6	10	20
VELASQUEZ	20	19	20	19	20	20	20	15	20
BOUGUEREAU	11	1	1	1	0	0	0	0	15
DALI	12	17	10	17	19	18	17	19	19
PICASSO	9	19	9	18	20	16	7	2	7
RAPHAEL	19	19	18	20	20	20	20	20	20
MANET	3	1	6	4	0	4	5	0	14
VERMEER DE DELFT	20	20	20	20	20	20	19	20	20
MONDRIAN	0	0	0	0	0	1	0,5	0	3,5

Dali's table for assessing the painters.

Dali and his contemporaries

Painters are generally isolated in a creative vacuum, with over-sized egos, and often hard put when asked to evaluate the work of their contemporaries. Dali is no exception to the rule. When asked for his overall opinion on contemporary art, he cries out loud and high: "Z E R O", a source of some considerable enmity ...

He "spits" on Cézanne, dubbing him with the charming nickname, the "impressionable" from Aix, and demolishes modern art, abstract art in particular, which he terms a "model of mental debility." He in fact considers that the followers of Kandinsky and Arp have led abstract art to a dead end. Architecturally speaking, he assassinates Le Corbusier and praises sky-high his compatriot Gaudi.

On the other hand, he rehabilitates Meissonier, a 19th century genre and battle painter and ceaselessly vaunts his three great Masters: Raphaël, Velázquez and Vermeer de Delft. The rare few spared are De Chirico, in whom he recognizes a certain influence on his century, Joan Miró, who helped him in his early days and who is also Catalan, and Braque, whose talent he praises but whose work he also calls "AR-CHE-O-LO-GY".

His painter friends (he does have a few), are Georges Mathieu, Tremois and Léonor Fini. As for Picasso, though he teases and sometimes has a dig, he can never forget being overblown by Picasso's talent when he met him in Paris in 1926. He recognizes in the latter a genius superior to his own, something in itself.

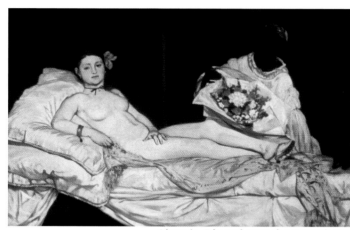

Olympia, **Edouard Manet's masterpiece that created a scandal in 1863.**

But Dali, surrealist and provocative in the extreme, does more than rant about other painters. He gives them all marks like simple Beaux-Arts students, and then publishes the notebook, "The Quarrel of Ancient and Modern Painters". In doing so he offends a great number of critics, museums and art institutions. But he reinforces the adulation of his ever-growing public, and in the long run, that is all that matters to him.

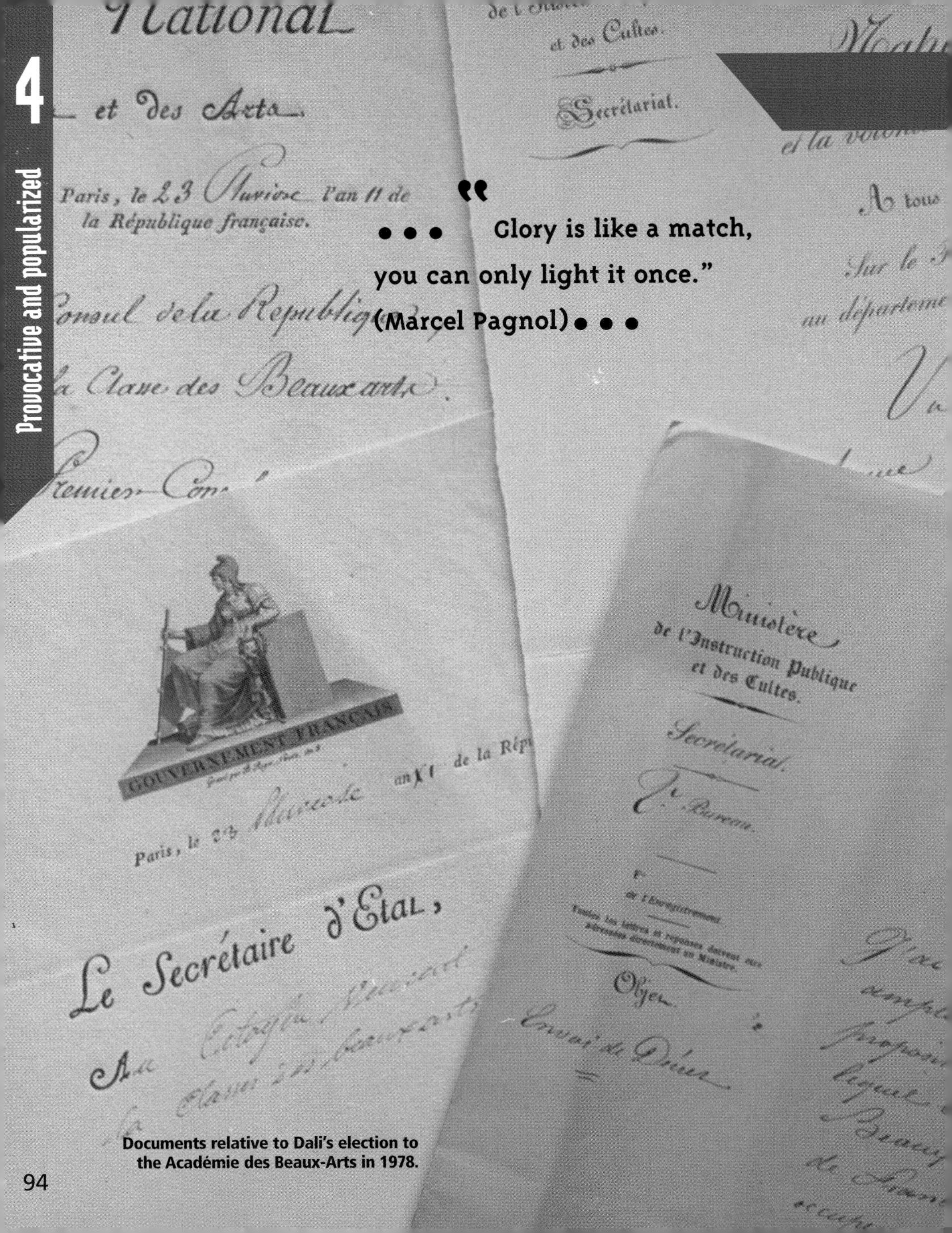

" **Glory is like a match,
you can only light it once."
(Marcel Pagnol)** ● ● ●

Documents relative to Dali's election to
the Académie des Beaux-Arts in 1978.

Official recognition

Dali is already sick and rather feeble when he sees himself elected to the French Académie des Beaux-Arts as foreign associate member in May 1978. And entering the institution necessitates some preparation which the Master does more or less willingly for nearly a year.

His entourage is a little circumspect about this belated homage, out of character with surrealist views, and designed principally to assure the presence of Dali and the gracious collaboration of collectors for a retrospective exhibition in preparation for the Pompidou Center. "You're the one honoring them by your presence and not the reverse," affirm certain friends.

The Master, a lover of disguise, sees in all this another occasion for fancy dress and a chance to stir up media attention by seeming to take himself seriously. So, on with the preparation. Multiple fittings for the elaborate costume for several months with a famous designer; a collection is organized amongst friends, as is customary, for the cost of manufacturing the sword that Dali

Dali and the painter Félix Labisse, president of the Académie des Beaux-Arts.

desires, in soft Toledo steel with a gold handle representing the face of Gala.

On the big day, May 9th, 1979, a surplus of invited guests creates a commotion worthy of a Persian market, but cannot prevent Gala, eighty-five years old, in a skintight Dior dress, from straddling banisters to get to her seat. Dali's secretary at the time forbids any live broadcasting of the event, having signed an exclusive contract with one channel, so cameras and microphones are not turned on.

Dali makes his entrance, two-cornered hat in hand, following an impressive line of immortals, to be welcomed by the President of this noble assembly and launches into his well-prepared opening speech: "Gala, Velasquez and the Golden Fleece." But, damn!, the Master has his notes all mixed up and gets lost. So he improvises as well as he can, losing himself somewhere in between the Fleece, Gala and the train station in Perpignan.

The Academy, keen to have a trace of the ceremony, has placed a tape recorder on Dali's lectern. But Dali thumps his fist so much from the beginning of his speech that the humble apparatus is quickly deactivated, recording nothing. Though Dali was immortalized that day, his investiture to the Academy was not at all.

. . . **M**agazine covers are forever

bandying the dandy with

a hallucinated look. But out of

the limelight, is an everyday Dali,

in places that he has chosen, with

his close friends, passions, doubts

and fears ● ● ●

5 In private

" **... I manufactured Dali, the greatest artist of our time, he became the Divine thanks to me, and that, for me, is enough" (Gala) ...**

Gala posing in a Dior dress in her house in Pùbol, in front of a door painted in trompe-l'œil.

Muse and supporter

Though a totally different type from her illustrious husband, Gala Dali is completely atypical of her time. With an exceptional personality, she is to the artistic milieu what Marie-Laure de Noailles is to the aristocratic world of the day.

Amuse with eyes like electric drills, she has the slimmest of waist-lines and a well-spoken voice, rolling her 'r's with a distinct Slavic accent. Her physical appearance, always impeccable, quickly hides the dozen years between her and Dali. She hates publicity, the media and cliques of any kind, declares herself to be without prejudice and has no problem in speaking her mind, be it with a slap in the face or a kick in the pants!

This behavior makes her seem caustic and disagreeable to many, especially since it is she who runs the business and finances of the Dali house-hold with an iron hand and no kid gloves. Some also criticize her for having turned her husband from his natural surrealist leanings towards more pious, conformist subjects.

Her role is however dominant. She shoulders, indefatigably, any number of tasks for her Divine husband. In addition to her role of wife and muse, she plays the mother who departed too soon, the chauffeur, the bodyguard, the model, the first critic of works in progress, the censor, the dealer, the secretary. The one and only person able to pinpoint Salvador Dali by comparing the man with the public persona, she never gives the key to the enigma.

At times exhausted by a shield too heavy to carry, she sometimes flies off to Italy or the French Riviera for amorous escapades with young, handsome companions. Reputedly a tough business woman, at these times, out of the spotlights, she spends lavishly and lets her mask fall.

Gala and Dali arriving in New York from Lisbon on August 17th, 1940 on the steamship *Excambion*.

Towards the end of her life, in order to flee a Port Lligat invaded by summer tourists, Gala has Dali buy the castle of Pùbol and decorate it for her. In the mountains, fiffty miles from Cadaquès, this place becomes her refuge and later her burial place. Her illustrious husband has the right to visit his muse here if he so wishes, but only with an expressly hand-written invitation from her. Dali accommodates himself very well to this situation, even admitting: "As the days go by, I become more and more masochistic, a condition I love."

"
• • •   Dali must be mesmerizing
himself into Cape Creus" **• • •**

**Dali taking a "noodle bath" in the
little bay of Port Lligat.**

Port Lligat

Let me see you at home, I'll tell you who you really are. No-one can truly understand Dali's roots until discovering the charm of Port Lligat, his stamping ground as a child, and where, from 1929 on, he lives with Gala, relatively undisturbed by the press for seven months of the year.

Astone's throw from Cadaquès, this little fishing village, tucked away in an inlet, is hard to reach by land. For years, the best access was by sea. Couched on the slopes of relatively barren mountains, its landscape ends with the austere rocks of Cape Creus.

Below vineyards tiered in espaliers, a little stone beach where a few fishing-boats lie in seeming abandon. The sea is often motionless. Its petrified, oily immensity coupled with a very particular wash of light, gives the impression of a fixed, timeless and rather nostalgic place.

Dali's home in Port Lligat, near Cadaquès, in Spain.

The Dalis reside here during the year from March to October in a conglomeration of tiny white-washed fishing-houses, bought one after the other and joined together, as success permitted. When the sea is calm, the couple take the boat out as far as Cap Creus and throw crayfish nets. Sea urchins are their favorite.

In the morning, the Master goes for a quiet swim, seen only by the swans that love this spot. The water looks doubtful, more like a swamp than the Mediterranean, a curious mixture of bird droppings, feathers and overgrown seaweed. Dali calls it his "noodle bath."

Dali's attachment to this place is visceral. These rocks, often painted by him, are second nature to him and the source of all the creative force and energy that he subsequently disperses cheerfully throughout the world. "Here I learn to delimit and refine my ideas," he says.

. . . **D**ali and Gala spend much of the year in the quiet of their home in Cadaquès • • •

Dali in the swimming-pool of his home in Cadaquès.

The nest

In 1930, a painting sold to the Vicomte de Noailles for twenty thousand francs allows the Dalis to buy a little white-washed fishing cabin in Port Lligat. Their only neighbor at the time is an ex-priest. Little by little, and on their return in 1948 from their American exile, they buy the adjoining cabins and connect them all together.

Gala's interior design is sober, almost monastic. In the entrance, a great bear greets visitors and doubles as a cane stand. A library garnished with several stuffed birds follows, its precious books placed on two high shelves deliberately out of reach, and a circular living-room garnished with low couches.

Then comes the atelier, relatively classical in design, prolonged by a little split-level space that the Master calls his "kitsch theater," decked with an assortment of paraphernalia from the Dalinian universe. The fact that the house has only one bedroom allows the couple to discreetly preserve their intimacy, obliging every visitor, important contacts and close friends alike, to stay at the nearby hotel.

Outside, lies a large terraced garden, sloping down from the cemetery wall at the top to a little jetty at the bottom. A patio, vast and very beautiful, is decorated with monumental teacups, a tiled horse-shoe table and a staircase which overlooks a niche containing two large eggs. A long cemented path called "The Milky Way" winds through the garden, past a stone throne in local marble on which Dali likes to be photographed.

The dovecote of Dali's home and the bay of Port Lligat.

Much further on, the decor includes a highly surrealist touch, a swimming-pool in the shape of a phallus with at one end a symbolic vagina, in the form of a half-moon niche made from the polystyrene wrapping of an old radio. A private pool meant for the exclusive use of the Divine Dali, the only one to crunch his feet on sea urchins embedded intentionally in the bottom …

" ••• There is always one moment in people's lives when they realize they adore me" •••

The "coach of the forgotten ones." Arturo Caminada, in a brown shirt, is climbing on.

Till death do us part

Dali is forever giving his opinion on anything and anyone when being interviewed or just fooling around. There are however a few rare people who, though they count enormously to him, are never mentioned. By deliberately putting his inner sanctum of faithful in the shade, he avoids misrepresenting them in any way.

Arturo Caminada, known to Dali's circle as faithful Arturo, a boy from Cadaqués introduced by a painter friend, begins to work for him at the age of seventeen. He becomes the chauffeur, the sailor, the servant and the gardener. He looks after the house while his masters are away, and during their seven months of the year in Port Lligat, takes care of their every need.

Always attentive and very discreet, when Gala dies in Port Lligat, he unhesitatingly wraps a blanket around her and takes her to the castle of Pùbol before announcing her decease. It is again Arturo who, each day of the seven years of his master's agony, drives the fifty miles from Cadaqués to Pùbol, and then another twenty from Figueres to his own village, just to keep an eye on him during this difficult time.

And it is also he who, in tears, places a white handkerchief over the face of his lifelong companion before closing the coffin, in respect of Dali's last wishes, which have been blithely ignored, for a private burial and a covered face. Faithful to the last, he passes away at the age of fifty-seven, in the year following his divine master's death.

One remembrance does exist of these unknown people. On a lovely day in 1971, Dali asks the photographer Marc Lacroix to immortalize his circle of faithful in Pùbol. Posing around a carriage with Gala in the driving-seat and Dali exceptionally relegated to the post of a simple footman, feature all those of whom the master is to say: "These, the most important people in my life, are known to no-one." Looking at the photo, Dali entitles it with gratitude the "coach of the forgotten ones."

Gala on the stairs of the castle of Pùbol.

105

❝ • • • The greatest ideas don't come in front of the Parthenon, the Venus of Milo, the Bay of Naples or the Niagara Falls. They come from insignificant sources: a boulevard, a tramway, a bathroom ... Each of us has his own train station in Perpignan" **• • •**

The Train Station in Perpignan, **Dali, 1965.**

The train station in Perpignan

Declared by the Divine Dali (with pseudo-scientific explanation) to be the "center of the world" in the 1960s and the subject of one of his most famous paintings, the train station in Perpignan is above all an important, ritual stopover, a transit lounge between creation and recreation.

In early autumn, after six quiet months of intense work in Port Lligat, Dali and Gala drive to Paris, the first stage of their recreational and promotional activities before getting down to business in New York in the winter.

The most recent paintings have to be shipped to both places, meaning an obligatory initial stop in Perpignan. Gala has to go through customs formalities before sending off the works. Dali waits on his own in the station for two or three hours. Like any artist about to exhibit recent creations, he wonders about his inspiration and his talent.

He buys lots of magazines, and leafs through

Perpignan, "center of the world" according to Salvador Dali.

them sitting on a bench, gradually relaxing. He begins to savor the dishes they will be eating in Valence and Saulieu. As he thinks up some wild ideas for France ... some extravagant costumes for America ...

Beneath the glass roof of the Perpignan train station, a mutation of two personalities is taking place. The painter and solitary creator is hiding until next spring behind the public figure.

"Suddenly there, in all the bustle of the arrival hall, in front of everyone, I am immobile, idle, experiencing intense pleasure, absolute bliss, an apotheosis, and a torrential ejaculation of ideas. For brusquely, and with colossal acuity, I see a vision of the painting I should have done, right down to the most minute detail, the painting I had been looking for all summer ..."

107

Dali in Port Lligat in 1955.

"••• A terrible coward, I am always afraid that things will backfire on me"•••

Un-shoeing the mask

Dali loved every exhibitionist moment, every chance his outrageous satire would get to send up all the symbols of our society. Knowing this, it seems hard to imagine that behind this provocative side, lies a sensitive, secret man, circumspect and shy to the point of timidity. And yet …

As a child he is terrified of insects, especially grasshoppers. Painting them into his work helps treat the phobia. As a young man, he thinks himself incapable of ever satisfying a woman. When he goes to a brothel with surrealist friends, he keeps his distance from the ladies, still not too sure how you catch venereal disease. So when Gala finds him in 1929, he is still a virgin, with a lot of preconceived ideas.

She quickly becomes his support, a rampart against the world, and manages to channel the madness with which he has a natural tendency to flirt. But if she, his muse in shining armor, as much as catches a virus or a bad attack of bronchitis, Dali ages ten years in one day. He knows, in fact, that without Gala, he is totally lost.

He acknowledges that he is a coward, and when friends go through hard times he swears he could never bear it himself. Both in his daily life and in his imaginary world, he lives in total insecurity. An object

Salvador Dali, the man with many faces, posing with a cane and a gold lion's head.

falling, a sudden darkness, or cries in a neighboring room make him jump for fright. He is quick to panic. Terrified of flying, he will only cross the Atlantic by sea. He never drives his old Cadillac himself.

When in May, 1968, the concierge of the Meurice Hotel warns him that a delegation of striking students want to talk to him, he is terrorized, imagining the worst. He enjoins his whole circle to stay and protect him if needs be. Just as four students, future doctors, rather intimidated, come into the suite and respectfully ask the Master for a contribution to their movement. Relieved to have got off so lightly, Dali writes them a very beautiful text in one night, *My Cultural Revolution*, distributed a few days later on the barricades.

❝ • • •   Captain, please show this lady out, she obviously ignores that at the court of the Divine Dali, we do not quarrel!" • • •

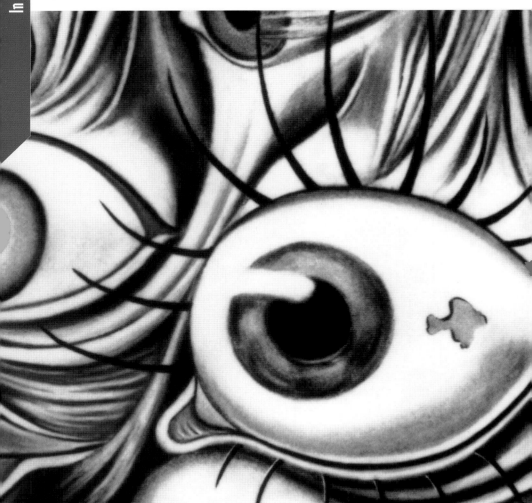

Dali and his sixth sense ...

A sixth sense

Getting into Dali's entourage means representing a solid intellectual, social or financial interest, and conforming to the codes and games played in this caravan of "deluxe Gypsies," a phrase coined by Captain Moore.

Used to moving in fashionable circles, the Master, a perfect gentleman, never forgets to kiss a lady's hand. He embraces male acquaintances because hand-shaking is not natural to him. Avid to learn and very curious by nature, he prefers by far to sound out others than tell stories about himself. This astonishes many a visitor who, having generally come to find out about Dali, finds himself at the end of the meeting having said all there was to say about himself, before being dispatched with the Master's ritual "Bonjour!"

Living as nomads for half the year in palace hotels, the couple mix with hundreds of people from different walks of life. The "chosen few" are selected instinctively and rites of passage generally over very quickly. Dali and Gala know how to open their intimate universe to a few, but they can also rid themselves unceremoniously of anyone in whom they sense potential betrayal or eventual disillusionment.

At the end of the 1960s, Dali's suite at the Meurice, is full of people. The Master is giving an interview (filmed by Gaumont) in one corner of the room, when a new group enters, along with a sixty-year-old dandy wearing light gray felt spats, buttercup-yellow gloves and holding a cane. A big art dealer from Brussels, he wants to meet the Master, hopefully on business.

Over the general commotion, the apartment telephone rings. Someone answers and gestures emphatically to the elegant old man that the call is for him. Very embarrassed, the latter nonetheless takes the receiver and goes into a rather long-winded explanation. From one end of the salon to the other, Dali who has missed nothing of the scene, stops his interview for a second, stares at the insolent offender with his beady eye and says in a very loud voice: "Mossieur, don't start selling for too much what is not yours to buy!" The final last words having been pronounced, exit the art dealer!

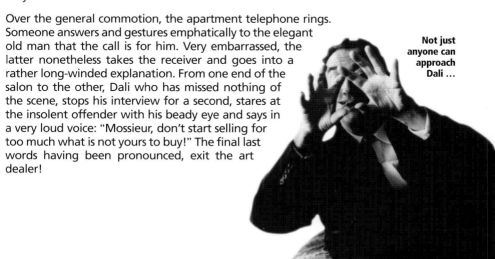

Not just anyone can approach Dali …

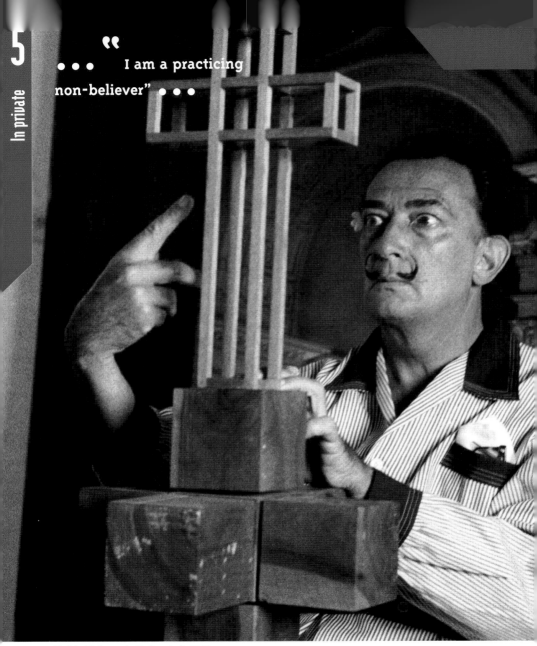

"... I am a practicing non-believer" ...

Dali in his home in Cadaquès in 1960.

Beliefs and superstitions

It is common knowledge that, when it comes to superstitions, the couple Gala-Dali usually see eye to eye. Dates, places to go and new friends are chosen only after having been subjected to criteria sometimes far from rational.

The number 13 is particularly popular with the couple and often chosen for Dalinian parties. While her husband is on show, Gala often has her tarot read by fortune-tellers, and continues to do so until she is quite elderly.

On one visit to friends, after having grumbled about one or two things as usual, Gala wanders off to the garden lawn where, more lovable and comely than ever, she begins to scrutinize attentively. Her hosts wonder why she doesn't seem to notice their flowers until, overjoyed, she returns triumphantly brandishing a bouquet of at least ten little green trophies for their benefit. For over an hour, she has been searching for four-leaf clover in the grass.

Dali's beliefs are more subtle but just as strong, plus he is always on the look-out for the workings of destiny. One morning at the Meurice, a present arrives. A precious book, bound in red morocco leather. The text is written in Catalan which is the reason for the present. The Master raises his eyes, opens the book, points a finger and looks down.

A fragment of an engraving illustrating Goethe's *Faust*, 1968. In the center, the cabalistic palindrome:

S	A	T	O	R
A	R	E	P	O
T	E	N	E	T
O	P	E	R	A
R	O	T	A	S

The word he is pointing at is "Cucurou." "Incredible!", exclaims Dali, "that's the name of the rock opposite the village where I was born!" Flabbergasted and carried away by the coincidence, he immediately calls up Gala, on holiday abroad, to tell her about it. After hanging up, he falls to his knees on the floor of the apartment with the murmur: "Picasso is still protecting me!", his fetish phrase whenever he wants to thank Almighty God.

"••• Today, science has become to the intelligence, a living shadow of faith" •••

Christ of Saint John of the Cross, **Dali, 1951.**

right:
Dali carrying his cross.

"Divine" views on God

Master Dali is always proclaiming himself to be "Catholic, apostolic and Roman." Though his family was not religious, and his father a free-thinker, in the course of his career he will often treat large-scale religious subjects with his own joyous blend of blasphemy and provocation. But therein lies all the ambiguity of his personality.

Very influenced for years by his father's library of numerous atheist and blasphemous works, the young Salvador, with his solid Cartesian and materialist mind, is not particularly attracted to the faith. Only later, after reading more widely, especially Nietzsche, and reflecting scientifically and philosophically, does he begin to feel doubt.

"An unbelieving Catholic, I make a detour through science to reach dogma," he declares. Continually buffeted between desire and reason, he would like to be able to believe in the resurrection of the flesh and the spirit, but the century's scientific certitudes finally prevent him doing so.

On a day to day basis, Dali uses religious questions mainly to shock middle-class mentalities. Each time an interviewer invariably broaches the subject of religion, he answers with a series of light-hearted quips like: "God is a mountain of Camembert cheese," "If God created the world in six days, I can take at least two minutes to speak of him," or "God is hardly larger than the tip of my cane."

Life works in more subtle ways for, apart from these blasphemous statements quite in keeping with his provocative persona, Dali leaves to posterity some very great religious masterpieces like *The Last Supper*, *The Madonna of Port Lligat* or *The Christ of Glasgow*. Perhaps in the end he adopted the approach of Voltaire: "God and I are not on speaking terms, but we do salute each other."

" ● ● ●   To say I think about death all the time is not enough. I wear its fabulous presence" ● ● ●

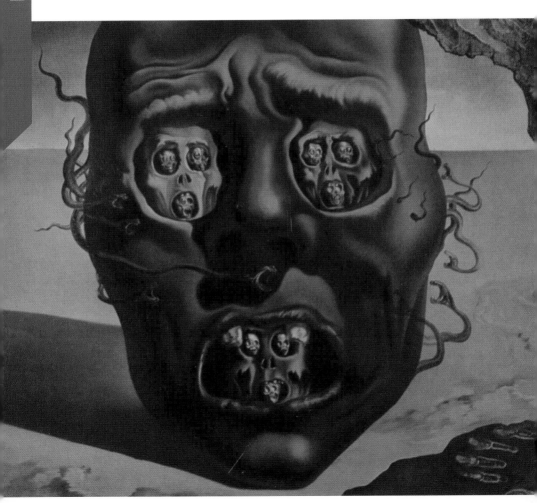

Visage of war, **Dali, 1940-41.**

Death

Not only omnipresent in his work, the theme of death preoccupies Dali's thinking throughout his life. Though he can manage to accept the fatality of his carnal envelope, he obstinately refuses to believe in the death of the soul or the spirit, and is prepared for any philosophical, scientific or religious detour to confirm his certitude.

His reaction to the death of others is quite particular. When he learns his friend Garcia Lorca has just been shot, his cry of funereal oration is "Olé". For him, the announcement of a close friend's death is digested in three stages: "First of all, I tell myself that I killed him. Then I reason with myself, persuading myself that this is not the case. Until I finally realize that this death, in being one hundred per cent Dalinian, reinforces my position as a living person and favors the birth of my work."

Bees, grasshoppers, young girls and knights abound in his painting. All symbols of death and decomposition, they permeate all Dali's major themes.

In some ways, he incorporates the death of others to exorcise his own. But he knows that in this game, however well he plays, he has no chance of winning. The inescapable still lies at the end of the road, no doubt explaining his creative bulimia and his continual need to do more.

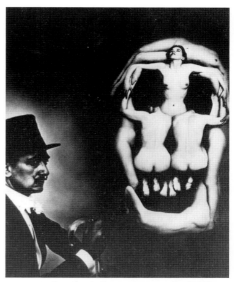

Dali posing before a photograph of Philippe Halsman, made in 1951, and based on one of his gouaches. The women's bodies are arranged to form a skull.

At the end of the 1960s, an impression that American research on the conservation of bodies in liquid helium is about to prove conclusive, gives him a ray of hope. Highly enthusiastic about the whole process, he is about to pay fifty thousand dollars to become the first 20th century genius reborn in the 21st century.

But he quickly realizes that this technique will not be able to be perfected for a long time. All he can do is await as best he can this terrible finality like an ordinary mortal. He makes just one ultimate request: "life in the afterworld with the persistence of memory."

" ● ● ● The most successful balls are the ones everyone talks about without ever going to" ● ● ●

The cuckold ball

Dali's decline, which begins -predictably- with the death of Gala in 1982 and finishes seven years later with the demise of the painter on January 23rd, 1989, is so dreadful and appalling, that it cannot figure among the fifty best stories of the Master.

Though there is humor to be found in the sinister choreography danced around a bedridden recluse by the macabre interests of States, governments, provinces and certain individuals. The most laboriously premeditated calculations and intrigues so often hit unforeseen obstacles.

Dali's main legacy are of course his works, but these have been lying dormant for ages in museums and private collections all over the world. The painter's liquid assets in American, Swiss and Spanish bank accounts have been frozen by God knows who from the beginning of the 1980s. Property assets of the Catalan do not amount to much.

Royalties could though. With no-one left to defend the image of a man and his work, the planet could be inundated with perfumes, ties, socks, t-shirts and other kitsch "dalicacies". Royalties therefore become the object of everyone's desire, and the pretext for a merciless battle for several years over Dali's agonizing body, reduced for the first time in his life to being a helpless spectator.

But that my passport be confiscated to make sure that I really do die in Spain, that I be sequestered, terrorized, and the world shown images of my dying, that I be forced to change my will, that I be buried in my museum instead of with my Muse, that I be looted, and counterfeited… all of this is nothing compared to the immense pleasure I have had, for nearly a century, the century of Dali, of "cuckolding" you all!

BON JOUR!

Dali in 1976, with Jean Christophe Argillet

Because Salvador Dali was so like an illusionist in seeming to reveal everything but always concealing the essential clues, it is practically impossible to know who he really was. Along with his numerous biographers and friends, I have also come to this same conclusion after having patiently studied his life and work.

The analysis of his friend, Michel Déon, a member of the Academy, written on the day following Dali's investiture in 1978, seems to me particularly pertinent:

"He is easy to take for a madman, because he says the most outrageous things with extraordinary common sense. All those who love him, and hold him to be a genius, or at the very least a great talent, would appreciate this absorbing man (now a member of the Academy) putting a stop to his antics. I would love to see him shave off those fangs, stop rolling those globular eyes, and stop exploiting the incredible fortuitousness of accident. He has had everything an artist could wish for. If only he would consent to no longer being a media star, his art would shine through and be seen as much greater. We would know his work to be one of the greatest of our time. But perhaps this is too much to ask of a man who has raised mystification to the level of a dogma."

To penetrate the intimacy of Dali, is to see the performer, the practical joker, the eternal kid having fun and preparing his next farce. Some people deplore him, esteeming that he loses energy, time and credibility with all his carrying on. They say it ruins his talent. Less categorical, I see the two sides of his personality as complementary and absolutely indispensable to each other.

Would he have talked as much about onanism if he had not painted *The Great Masturbator*? Or inversely, would he have ever painted *The Train Station in Perpignan* without experiencing there a veritable epiphany?

On a cold sunny afternoon in February, 2004, I was sitting below his house in the little bay of Port Lligat, in the landscape that had been his for over fifty years, when two important points suddenly hit me.

This bay, very small in size and closed off from the sea, gives the impression of a world in miniature, sufficient unto itself. Everything is here: water, land, sky and rock, in a single unit. It is a pocket universe, as hard to leave as the frame of one of the Master's paintings. Finding myself alone and lost in thought was like finding myself immersed in one of his works.

Conclusion

Dali was painting the scenery he had before his eyes every day, without forgetting of course two major elements: his immense talent and his surrealism. Why paint anything else when in an essential microcosm like this where nothing has been left out?

The second point was a need he must have felt to get out of this enclosure, oppressive in the long run, and delve into its opposite. New York and Paris are in essence a negation of Port Lligat. Dali needed a life between two opposites to find force and balance. On the one hand, creative calm to fashion his art and, on the other, indispensable recreation to manufacture his public persona and exploit his paranoia. His force and complexity lies in this clever combination.

But his personality lies essentially in one simple principle: being superior to everything around him. Extraordinarily charismatic, he glides over any assembly, any subject, any difficulty. Try to trap him and with a graceful maneuver he will always fall on his feet. Scientists, artists, politicians, philosophers or artisans are all charmed by the Master, and astonished at his encyclopedic, revolutionary knowledge.

An insatiable, relentless worker, we can wonder at how in a single lifetime he managed to create so many works, scenarios, and at the same time travel so much, be so constantly provocative, behind so many happenings, give interviews, do television advertisements, and still balance this intense social life with a private life.

When old age, illness, and Gala's death, finally prevent him from leading this great surrealist ball, everything begins to go downhill. Nature had given him everything: Love, Genius and Fame. Did she come at the end of his life to counterbalance all her gifts? In any case, the Dali system, one we would have liked to have seen as infallible, collapses and no-one can do anything.

The man disappears. A page turns. But as a result, the work of this unparalleled designer, meticulous engraver and limitlessly imaginative painter comes to the surface. It is high time that the name of Dali immediately bring to mind one of his masterpieces rather than a rebellious moustache and a flashy look.

For his entire life, Dali struggled with his own demons. The first, death itself, he has partly conquered, in bequeathing to posterity so many masterpieces. Only three or four would have sufficed to make him infinitely famous.

The mountain of works he leaves to our judgement is considerable, "chef-d'oeuvral" as he used to say. Now, over a centenary after his birth, it stands waiting to be discovered and rediscovered, and is still far from revealing all its secrets.

Appendixes

1894

Elena Ivanovna Diakonova is born in Kazan (Russia), the daughter of a high Muscovite official.

1904

Salvador Dali is born on May 11th, in Figueres (Spain).

1913

Diagnosed with tuberculosis, Elena is sent to the sanatorium of Clavadel (Switzerland) where she meets Paul Eluard.

1917

Elena and Paul Eluard marry. He nicknames her Gala and presents her to the Parisian surrealist circle made up of Max Ernst, René Magritte, André Breton, etc. Gala becomes their muse.

1918

Dali's first exhibition in Figueres is favorably reviewed.

Birth of Cécile, daughter of Gala and Paul Eluard.

1921

Dali's mother dies. In October he goes to the San Fernando Beaux-Arts Academy, in Madrid. Becomes friends with Luis Buñuel and Federico Garcia Lorca.

1923

Imprisoned for 35 days for heading a student riot. Expelled for one year from San Fernando for having questioned the authority of his teachers.

1926

April, Dali's first trip to Paris where he meets Picasso. In October, definitively expelled from the Madrid Beaux-Arts Academy.

1928

Second trip to Paris where Dali meets the surrealists.

1929

Gala, then Mrs. Paul Eluard and Salvador Dali meet in Cadaquès. Paul Eluard returns alone to Paris. Production with Buñuel of *Un Chien andalou*, Dali's ticket into the surrealist group.

1932

Paintings are sent to New York for the first surrealist retrospective.

1934

Excluded from the surrealists because of his divergent artistic and political views.

Chronology Dali-Gala

1938

International surrealist exhibition in Paris. Meets Sigmund Freud.

1939

Exhibits for the first time in New York.

1940

Gala and Dali remain in exile in New York until 1948. "Classical" and "Renaissance" period.

1950-60

They return to Europe. "Mystical" period. Three dimensional paintings.

1959

Presentation in Paris of the "ovociped", a Dalinian invention.

1963

Release of *Diary of a genius*.

1966-1970

Two major paintings: *Tuna fishing* (1966-67) and *The hallucinating toreador* (1969-70).

1970

Dali buys Gala the castle of Pùbol (Spain) where she will often stay.

1978

Decorated with the Great Cross (the highest Spanish distinction) and elected to the French Beaux-Arts Academy as foreign associate.

1982

On June 10th, death of Gala. When the news is announced to Dali, he says: "she is not dead, she will never die."

1983

Creation of Dali perfumes, a bottle in the shape of lips for women, and in the shape of testicles for men. Dali paints his last work.

1984

Dali is very badly burnt in a fire that breaks out in his bedroom.

1989

January 23rd, death of Dali. In his will, he bequeaths his property and his works to the Spanish State.

André Breton

André Breton, the dictatorial leader of the surrealists, opens the doors of the group to the young Salvador Dali. Later, their relationship is compromised by their artistically, and more especially, politically divergent views.

Born in Tinchebray in the department of the Orne on February 18th, 1896, he spends his childhood in Pantin, in the Paris region. At the age of eighteen, he begins to study medicine, and publishes three poems, one dedicated to Paul Valéry, which appear in the magazine *La Phalange*.

During WW I, he serves in the medical corps. He becomes interested in psychoanalysis and meets Guillaume Apollinaire. The latter introduces him to Aragon and Philippe Soupault. In 1919, these three launch *Littérature*, a magazine of experimental writing with Dadaist tendencies. The same year, he publishes *Mount of piety*, a work in which he distances himself from the poetry of Mallarmé, and *Magnetic Fields*, co-written with Soupault, the fruit of the practice of automatic writing. In 1924, Breton marries Simone Khan. After the break with Tristan Tzara and the Dada movement in 1922, Breton and his group turn towards surrealism, expounding its basic tenets with their famous *Surrealist Manifesto* in 1924. From then on, Breton assumes the leadership of the surrealist movement. A meeting in 1926 with a certain Nadja inspires an eponymous work, distilled with all the major themes of surrealism (love, dreams, the relationship of life to poetry).

A militant communist from 1927, Breton is excluded from the party for his divergent views on culture in 1935, views which will also distance him from Aragon. During this period he writes the *Second Manifesto of Surrealism* and *The Communicating Vases*, reflections on what art should be. In 1934, his meeting with Jacqueline Lamba inspires *Mad love*. Four years later, during lectures he gives in Mexico, he becomes friends with Trotsky and writes with him the manifesto: *For Independent Revolutionary Art*. He breaks with Paul Eluard.

In 1941, after the French defeat, Breton leaves for Martinique where he meets Aimé Césaire, and then moves to New York where he participates in the surrealist exhibition of 1942. In 1946, remarried to Elisa, he returns to Paris. The aftermath of the war is the occasion for him to fight for the independence of Vietnam and then of Hungary, controlled by the USSR. During the war in Algeria, he is one of the first to sign the *Manifesto of the 121* against the war. André Breton dies on September 28th, 1966. His death notice reads simply:

ANDRE BRETON
1896-1966
J'ai cherché l'or du temps
(I searched for the gold of time)

Luis Buñuel

Luis Buñuel and Salvador Dali met while studying in Madrid and made their first film together. For Luis Buñuel, this is the beginning of a fantastic movie career ...

Born in Calanda (Aragon, Spain), Luis Buñuel, was the eldest of seven. From a middle-class family, he had a strict religious education. At the age of seventeen, he goes to study in Madrid where he meets Dali, Garcia Lorca and joins the Dadaist movement. In 1925, he leaves for Paris. Increasingly attracted by cinema, it is Fritz Lang's *The three lights* which finally inspires him to become a director. A student of cinema, he works in 1928 on the shooting of *The Fall of the House of Usher*. At the same time he experiments with writing scenarios and founds a cinema club at the university of Madrid. This same year, 1928, he makes his first feature with Dali, *Un Chien andalou*. The film, acclaimed by the surrealists, marks their entrance into the group.

Two years later, in 1930, *L'Age d'Or* creates a scandal and Luis Buñuel leaves to spend a few months in Hollywood. Based mainly in the States, he begins a prolific career as director, editor, embassy attaché. Marxist, anarchist and anti-clerical, he is finally obliged to move to Mexico, where he continues his career with notably *Los Olivados, The criminal life of Archibald de la Cruz, Death in the garden*. In these films, he deliberately shocks with an often violent, death-orientated, surrealist universe, where linear temporality is done away with. In 1961, scandal reoccurs with *Viridiana*, a spectacular denunciation of Spanish religious taboos. Several masterpieces follow ... *Tristana, Belle de jour, The exterminating angel, Diary of a Chambermaid*. In 1972, he receives an Oscar for *The Discreet Charm of the Bourgeoisie. This obscure object of desire*, in 1977, is his last film. He dies on July 29th, 1983 in Mexico.

Michel Déon

The surrealists were not the only literary figures to associate with Dali. He undertook to write *The secret life of Salvador Dali* with Michel Déon, author and journalist.

Michel Déon was born in Paris on August 4th, 1919. His family were in the military and the public service. Before the war, he studied law. Initially called up, after his demobilization in 1942, he worked as an editor for *L'Action française* and other magazines, as he was writing his first novel.

In 1950, American sponsorship allowed him to go to the United States to study the language of the Cajun in Louisiana. On his return to France, he began to publish novels, becoming literary advisor for Plon editions in 1956. He was awarded two literary prizes, in 1951, the "Prix de la Ville de Nice" for *Je ne veux jamais l'oublier* (*I never want to forget*) and in 1954, the "Prix des Sept" for *Le Dieu pâle* (*The pale God*). He then collaborated with the publishing house La Table Ronde, while working as a literary critic. From 1969 on, he spent his time between Greece, Ireland and Paris. He continued to receive a series of prizes: the "Prix Interallié" for *The wild ponies* in 1970, the "Grand Prix" from the French Academy for his novel *A mauve taxi*, and the European prize for children's literature in 1976 for *Thomas and the infinite*. In 1996, he was awarded the Prix Giono for the entire body of his work.

Michel Déon was elected to the Académie Française on June 8th, 1978.

Paul Eluard

The poet Paul Eluard and Dali are first united by a common interest in surrealism. They meet when Dali is on a trip to Paris. But a few years later, Eluard and Dali are to have something else in common: Gala ...

Paul Eugène Grindel, born in 1895 in Saint-Denis is the son of a banker and a dress designer. A gifted student, he catches tuberculosis in 1912 and has to interrupt his studies to convalesce in the Clavadel sanatorium in Switzerland. There he meets Gala, a young woman from Russia, with whom he falls in love. He writes his first poems. In 1914, Paul Eluard is called up and sent to the front as a nurse. What he witnesses there, will mark his whole life and inspire in 1916 a book of poems, *Le Devoir* (*Duty*), in which he expresses his horror of war. For the first time, he signs as Paul Eluard, his grandmother's maiden name.

In 1917, he marries Gala, his muse, also later to become the muse of the surrealist group (composed of André Breton, Louis Aragon and Philipppe Soupault), when he joins them in 1919 after the release of his *Poems for peace*. The following year, Eluard launches his periodical *Proverbe* in which he collaborates with the Dadaists. Like most surrealists, Eluard is interested in the graphic arts and experimental literature but he also shows great admiration for classical poetry. In 1926, inspired by his turbulent relationship with Gala, he publishes one of his most famous collections of verse, *Capitale de la douleur* (*Capital of pain*). Three years later, Gala leaves him for Dali. Eluard then meets a young woman from Alsace called Nusch who inspires many love poems like *L'Amour, la poésie* (*Love, poetry*) or *La vie immédiate* (*The immediate life*). Excluded in 1933 from the Communist Party over a difference of opinion, Eluard continues to lobby for poetry accessible to all. His work is marked by very simple, highly metaphorical writing.

World War II gives Eluard the occasion to engage in the French Resistance. He clandestinely publishes *Le livre ouvert* (*The open book*) and *Poésie et Vérité* (*Poetry and Truth*). His poem Liberty is parachuted behind enemy lines. Nusch's death after the war leaves Eluard in despair: he publishes *Le temps déborde* (*Time runs over*). However, three years later, he meets Dominique, his third and last muse. She inspires his last love poems in a book of verse called *The Phoenix*. Seriously ill, Paul Eluard has enough time to publish one last work, *Sentiers et routes de la poésie* (*Paths and roads of poetry*), before dying on November 18th, 1952 at the age of 57.

Federico Garcia Lorca

A great friend of Dali, the Spanish poet met him when they were both students in Madrid. The two men seldom worked together but their respective works are both marked by Catholicism and the recurring themes of desire and death.

Federico Garcia Lorca was born in 1898 in the province of Grenada, in Andalusia. His father was a musician, his mother a school-teacher. Garcia Lorca grew up with many young gypsy friends and this culture was to impregnate his works. His literary and musical talent appears at a young age. In 1918, on a trip to Castille, he publishes his first book, *Impressions and Landscapes*. He meets Salvador Dali a year later at the university hostel in Madrid. They become very close friends.

In 1921, after the failure of his first play, Lorca publishes verse and organizes a competition of *cante jondo* (Andalusian singing). In 1927, his play *Mariana Pineda* is premièred with actress Margarita Xirgu in the title role. The following year is released a book of verse evoking the great epics of Andalusia, *The gypsy ballads*. Lorca is now famous in Spain. In 1929 and 1930, he lectures in Cuba and in the United States. Back in Spain, he devotes himself to writing. His work is marked by Andalusian and gypsy culture, melancholy, passion and death.

The institution of the Republic in 1931 allows him to form his own theatre group, "La Barraca", a State-financed itinerant troupe which enables the illiterate populations of Spain to access for the first time the great classical works. In 1933, his play *Blood wedding*, a violent love-story about honor and death, is a triumph in all Spanish-speaking countries. This work is followed in 1936 by a second installment, *Yerma*. Part of a theater trilogy, it is violently attacked by the extreme right.

The death of a toreador friend then inspires Lorca to write *Eulogy for the toreador Ignacio Sanchez Mejias*. In 1936, he finishes his trilogy with *The House of Bernarda Alba*. When the Popular Front that Lorca supports, takes power in Spain just before the Spanish Civil War, he is in Grenada. Arrested for his political sympathies by partisans of Franco, he is shot without trial on August 19th, 1936.

Georges Mathieu

Like his friend Salvador Dali, Georges Mathieu is an audacious, versatile artist who also turns his talent to architecture and publicity.

Georges Mathieu was born in Boulogne-sur-Mer on January 27th, 1921. After studying law, literature and philosophy, he becomes an English teacher in 1943. He paints his first oil paintings at this time. Three years later, he exhibits in the Paris Salon for artists under thirty, an event he helps to organize. He demands an art freed from all formal and aesthetic constraints, an art he calls "lyrical abstraction". Parallel to his artistic engagements, he has a brilliant professional career as editor of the *United States Lines Review*.

He paints his first so called "tachiste" works in 1950 but only becomes famous internationally from 1954. In the 1960s, keen to see art adding harmony to human life, he begins to create furniture, jewelry and publicity posters. An outspoken partisan for a utilitarian humanist education system in which the artist has a role to play, he becomes a member of a commission for the reform of France's Ministry of Education. He also participates in the construction of Castellaras, a new village in the Var. Georges Mathieu then explores monumental sculpture, notably for the sports complex in Neuilly.

Georges Mathieu has had over one hundred and fifty individual exhibitions throughout the world and four important retrospectives.

Louis Pauwels

A journalist and author, Louis Pauwels knew Dali very well. He published in 1989, a book of conversations and memories based on his intimate relationship to the artist.

Born in Paris in 1920, he was trained as a chemist. Louis Pauwels was a member of the French Resistance during the war, and deported to the camp of Mathausen. After the Liberation, he was a reporter for the newspaper *Combat*. He then contributed to the magazine *Arts*, before becoming director of the magazine *Marie-France*. Fascinated by scientific mystery, he published in 1961 with Jacques Berger a book called *The morning of the magicians* which had an overnight success. He then created *Planète*, a magazine which had an initial success but which ceased to appeal in the aftermath of May 68.

Louis Pauwels then disappeared for several years before returning in 1977 on the cultural staff of *Le Figaro*. He created a weekly version of the latter called *Le Figaro magazine* which soon became a success. A brilliant journalist, his intransigent views on matters of immigration and his adherence to a "new Right" preaching racial inequality did him great disservice. He remained director of *Figaro magazine* until 1993, four years before his death.

Pablo Picasso

Dali, often severe with regard to his contemporaries, confessed all his life to a great admiration for Picasso, whose genius he considered superior to his own.

Pablo Picasso, is born in Malaga (Spain) on October 25th, 1881. His father is a drawing teacher. From the age of twelve, he exhibits his first sketches and at the age of fourteen, attends the Beaux-Arts in Barcelona where his father has just been appointed. In 1897, he wins the gold medal at the Beaux-Arts exhibition in Malaga and is admitted, like Dali twenty years later, to the Royal San Fernando Academy in Madrid, which he never attends. Between 1900 and 1902, he goes several times to Paris, where he meets Max Jacob. On his second trip, his friend Casagemas commits suicide. Picasso paints the burial. This is the beginning of the blue period. In 1905, begins the rose period, when Picasso settles definitively in Paris. He discovers primitive art, which leads him towards a more refined style of which the first example is *Les demoiselles d'Avignon* in 1927. The bodies are fragmented, deformed, geometrical. Cubism is born. From 1912, the artist incorporates objects into some of his paintings: pieces of oilcloth, paper … After a short, more classical spell due to his collaboration with Diaghilev and his marriage to a Russian ballerina, in 1925 Picasso brusquely launches into the representation of dislocated bodies in violent colors, pleasing to the surrealists. In 1937, during the Spanish Civil War, a painting is commissioned from an already famous Picasso by the Spanish government. This becomes *Guernica*, one of his many masterpieces.

1940 is a prolific year for Picasso. He writes a play; *Desire caught by the tail*, and makes a famous sculpture, *Man with a sheep*. In between, other muses have taken the place of his wife Olga: Marie-Thérèse Walter, the photographer Dora Maar and Françoise Gilot. For several years, bullfighting has become one of his favorite themes. In 1948, as he begins ceramic work, a rich bestiary appears with a predominant motif being the Minotaur and the bull. However, it is a dove, painted in 1949 for the poster of the world peace conference, that becomes his most famous emblem.

Pïcasso spent the last twenty years of his life in Cannes and Mougins with his last wife Jacqueline. In 1955, he works on Clouzot's film *The Picasso Mystery* and repaints several large 19th century works. In May 1970, a huge Picasso retrospective in Avignon retraces sixty years of creation.

Picasso died on April 8th, 1973.

Pierre-Yves Tremois

One of the artists who had a chance to work with Dali, was Pierre-Yves Tremois, a painter and engraver less well-known to the general public, but highly respected in the artistic milieu.

Pierre-Yves Tremois, born in Paris on January 8th, 1921, studied at the Beaux-Arts in Paris. He was quick to distinguish himself, winning the Grand Prix de Rome for painting in 1943. With his own particular, easily identifiable style, he illustrates for important editing houses, many great works by authors like Mallarmé, Claudel or Montherlant. In 1961, he works on *The Apocalypse of Saint John*, in collaboration with Georges Mathieu, Zadkine and … Salvador Dali. Pierre-Yves Tremois' works include paintings, engravings, sculpture, ceramics and jewelry. He made a trophy for the Paris Opera and created the sword for Louis Pauwels when the latter entered the Académie Française. His paintings and creations are exhibited throughout the world since the 1960s. He was elected to the Academy of the Beaux-Arts in 1978.

Andy Warhol

Dali, very critical of abstract art, had a soft spot for pop art and for its most famous exponent, Andy Warhol, who had moreover, a "Dalinian" fascination with death.

From a modest family of Slovak immigrants, Andrew Warhola was born in Pittsburgh (USA) in 1928. After having studied graphic design at the Carnegie Institute of Technology in Pittsburgh, he begins to work in advertising as a graphic artist in 1949. In the 1940s, he is fascinated by politics and the transformation of American society. Very quickly, he upsets the world of publicity with his extraordinary packaging and record covers. He works for magazines like *Vogue*, *Glamour*, and for the *New York Times*. He achieves overnight advertising fame when he creates fifty innovative shoe designs in twenty-four hours for *Glamour*. In 1960, he begins to paint scenes from Popeye and Dick Tracy cartoons before realizing that market-orientated society can be a source of inspiration.

He then begins to use the imagery of different labels and ordinary mass-produced objects as a basis for serigraph prints on canvas. Andy Warhol justifies this principle of serigraphy by affirming that his paintings should be able to be made by a machine as easily as by himself. A fervent collector, he assembles rococo furniture, lamps, hundreds of cheap little gadgets and thousands of shoes of diverse shapes and sizes.

He then works from portraits of Marilyn Monroe and Elizabeth Taylor. Fascinated by death, he concentrates on the theme of the American dream in 1963 by composing paintings depicting riots or executions. His studio turns into a factory line where tens of people are employed to manufacture his creations in series.

From 1968 to 1972, Andy Warhol makes movies in which a great part is devoted to improvisation. He makes *Kiss*, *Empire*, *Chelsea Girls* and does portraits of celebrities like Mick Jagger or Mao Tse Tung. In the 1980s, his works reach astronomical figures. The most intransigent personality of pop art, he is the figurehead of New York *Underground*. Until his death in 1987, he helps to launch the young generation of New York artists. In 1990, a Warhol retrospective at the Pompidou Center attracted over 300,000 visitors.

The Dali Theater-Museum of Figueres

Inaugurated in 1974, the **Dali Theater-Museum** was built upon the remains of the former Figueres theater. At the end of the 1960s, as Dali was beginning to explore the project of a museum, the municipality of Figueres offered him the Municipal theater, still in ruins since being bombed out during the Spanish Civil War. "Where should be constructed my most extravagant and most solid work, if not in my own home town? The Municipal theater, or rather what was left of it, seemed perfect to me for three reasons: firstly, because I am an extremely theatrical painter; secondly because the Theater is just in front of the church where I was baptized; and lastly, because it was in the lobby of this very Theater that I had my first ever painting exhibition."

The museum retraces the artistic career of Salvador Dali (1904-1989) with a wide range of works, spanning from his earliest artistic experiments, impressionist, futurist and cubist, through his creations within the surrealist movement, to his last works. A reflection of his aesthetic extravagance, the **Dali Theater-Museum** has to be seen as a whole, as a great work of Salvador Dali, for everything in it was conceived and designed by the artist in order to offer visitors a chance to penetrate his captivating and unique world.

Address : Teatre-Museu Dali
Plaça Gala-Salvador Dali
E-17600 Figueres
Tel. (00 34) 725 118 00
www.figueresciutat.com or **www.salvador-dali.org**

July to September 9.00 a.m. to 7.45 p.m.
Visitors are allowed into the museum until 7.15 p.m.
Open every day, without exception.

January to June / October to December 10.30 a.m to 5.45 p.m.
Visitors are allowed into the museum until 5.15 p.m.

Closing days : 1 January, 25 December and Mondays (except bank holidays and on the eve of bank holidays).

Works written by Dali

The Conquest of the Irrational
New York: Julien Levy, 1935.

The Secret Life of Salvador Dali,
London: Vision Press, 1948.

Diary of a genius,
New York: Doubleday, 1965.

Lettre ouverte à Salvador Dali,
Albin Michel, 1966.

Dali by Dali,
New York: Abrams, 1970.

Hidden Faces,
New York: William Morrow, 1974.

Les Cocus du vieil art moderne,
Grasset, 1974.

Oui,
Gonthier, 1979.

Journal d'un génie adolescent,
Editions du Rocher, 2000.

The passions according to Dali,
St. Petersburg: Salvador Dali Museum,
1985.

Select bibliography

Reference sources on Dali

Ajame Pierre, *La double vie de Salvador Dali*, Ramsay, 1989.

Bosquet Alain, *Conversations with Dali*, New York: E. P. Dutton, 1969.

Descharnes Robert
Salvador Dali, The Work, The Man,
New York: Abrams, 1984.

Parinaud, André, *The Unspeakable Confessions of Salvador Dali*,
New York: Quill, 1981.

Pauwels Louis, *Dali m'a dit*,
Carrère, 1989.

Puget Henri, *L'Oeil de la folie*,
Jean Bouly, 1989.

Romero Luis, *Dali*,
Secaucus, NJ: Chartwell Books, 1979.

Catalogues

Catalogue raisonné of Dali's etchings (1924-1980), Prestel, Munich, 1994.

Salvador Dali, retrospective 1920-1980,
Centre Pompidou, Paris, 1980.

La vie publique de Salvador Dali,
Centre Pompidou, Paris, 1980.

Salvador Dali,
Tate Gallery, London, 1980.

Websites of Dali museums throughout the world:

www.salvador-dali.org

The official site of the Gala-Dali Foundation which runs the three Spanish museums (Figueres, Cadaquès , Port Lligat). Biographies, collections on line, Dalinian news and virtual visits of the three museums.

www.salvadordalimuseum.org

The site of the Dali Museum in Saint Petersburg (Florida). A presentation of the museum and its collection bequeathed by Eleanor and Reynolds Morse, news, visit on line.

www.figueresciutat.com

Site of Figueres in Spain, the artist's hometown, page devoted to the Dali Museum of Figueres.

www.cbrava.com

Spanish site devoted to the Costa Brava (Spain). Some information on the museum of Cadaquès (Port Lligat).

www.daliphoto.com

A rich collection of photos of Salvador Dali by Robert and Nicolas Descharnes.

Sites on the life and works of Dali:

www.dali-gallery.com

Salvador Dali Art Gallery. Site devoted to Dali and surrealism. Life and work of the painter, several hundred objects and paintings on line. A large section on surrealism with many links. Shop on line.

Internet resources

www.3d-dali.com

Biographies of Dali and Gala, many works on line with commentaries, technical explanation, criticism, selections of books and shopping on line.

Timée-Editions can not be held responsible for the content of these sites.

The Century of Dali on the web

Timée Editions offer readers a selection of some of the 50 best stories in French of Salvador Dali on the internet.

A few other stories and some surprises at:
www.timee-editions.com

Click on the book : *Le siècle de Dali*

Login : dali

Password : gala

"Timée-Editions — Open books on the internet"

The Timée Group is also :

Cultural events on line : www.zestory.com

Teaching materials on line : www.timee-education.com

A consulting agency and multimedia creation : www.timee-multimedia.com

Table of contents

Photography credits

Corbis agency : pp. 19, 20, 21, 22, 28, 30, 35, 39, 42, 44, 47, 53, 54, 58, 61, 65, 68, 69, 74, 75, 77, 79 (bas), 80, 85, 86, 87, 88, 89, 90, 91, 93, 94, 95, 99, 107, 108, 110

Gamma : 48, 49, 60, 64, 83 et 103.

Magnum : pp. 12 (Halsman), 34 (Halsman), 62 (Gauny) et 76 (Halsman).

Descharnes / Daliphoto.com : pp. 13, 14, 15, 16, 24, 25, 38, 55, 66, 81.

Marc Lacroix : pp. 18, 36, 37, 98, 102, 104 et 105.

Argillet : 23, 46, 57, 100, 101, 109 et 111.

Francesc Catalá-Roca : p. 115.

Pierre Boulat : p. 3.

DR : pp. 6, 17, 29, 31, 32, 33, 40, 41, 43, 45, 52, 56 (Jean Weber), 59 (Agnaci), 63, 67, 70, 71 (Giovanni Coruzzi), 78, 79 (haut), 82, 84, 92, 112, 113, 114, 116, 117

Editor
Laurent Tranier

Editorial assistants
Camille Armand
Sylvie Laffon

Graphic conception
Sylvain Kaslin

Graphic artist
Marc Charbit - Agence M
27 bis, rue Jules David
93260 Les Lilas

Layout
David Panzo - Graph'âme
159, rue Robespierre
93170 Bagnolet

Printing
E3 Expansion
28, rue des Tilleuls
92100 Boulogne – France

Timée-Editions
66, rue Escudier
92100 Boulogne – France
www.timee-editions.com

In the same collection
(other titles available only in French)

Sport and Leisure

Vert passion
Les 50 plus belles histoires de l'Association
Sportive de Saint-Etienne
Christophe Barge et Laurent Tranier

Le Tour de France, 100 ans de passion
Les 100 plus belles histoires du Tour de France
Eric Delanzy

L'Aventure des Bleus
Les 50 plus belles histoires de l'Equipe de France
de football
Alain Mercier

La passion de l'Olympisme
Les 50 plus belles histoires des Jeux Olympiques
Paul Miquel

Renault, la course en tête
Les 50 plus belles histoires de Renault en sport
Robert Puyal

Terre battante
Les 50 plus belles histoires de Roland Garros
Patrice Dominguez

Zidane, maître du jeu
Les 50 plus belles histoires de Zinédine Zidane
Étienne Labrunie

Science and Discovery

Les plus belles histoires des Trains
Les 50 plus belles histoires de l'épopée du chemin
de fer
Collectif

Les Aventuriers de l'Energie
Les 100 plus belles histoires de l'électricité
Nicolas Viot

Des Métaux et des Hommes
Les 50 plus belles histoires de la chaudronnerie
Louise Haroun

Dans les pas des Bâtisseurs
Les 50 plus belles histoires des bâtisseurs
Xavier Bezançon

History of Civilization

La folie Carnaval
Les 50 plus belles histoires du carnaval
Sarah Belabes

Le cœur des femmes
Les plus belles histoires des 50 femmes
du XXᵉ siècle
Roselyne Febvre

Sous le sable des arènes
Les 50 plus belles histoires de la corrida
François-Xavier Gauroy

La Liberté venue des Mers
Les 60 plus belles histoires de la Libération
de la France
Catherine Trouiller et Sharon Elbaz

Winston Churchill
Les 50 plus belles histoires de Winston Churchill
Denis Lépée

Le français en partage
Les 50 plus belles histoires de la francophonie
Christophe Traisnel
Préface : Abdoulaye WADE

Indiens, les premiers Américains
Les 50 plus belles histoires des Indiens d'Amérique
du nord
Fabrice Delsahut

Arts and Culture

Cannes fait son Cinéma
Les 50 plus belles histoires du Festival de Cannes
Nathalie Cuman

Jules Verne, le poète de la science
Les 50 plus belles histoires sur Jules Verne
Sous la direction de Jean-Paul Dekiss

Coups de foudre
Les 50 plus belles rencontres amoureuses
François-Xavier Gauroy

L'esprit du Vin
Les 50 plus belles histoires du Vin
Claude Chapuis

Les mille visages de Sartre
Les 50 plus belles histoires sur Jean-Paul Sartre
Sophie Richardin

To be released

Sport and Leisure

Entrez dans la légende
Les 50 plus belles histoires du Stade de France
Alain Billouin

Science and Discovery

La nature dans tous ses états
Les 50 plus belles histoires de l'environnement
Guersende Nagy

Arts and Culture

Jeux vidéos
Les 50 plus belles histoires des jeux vidéos
Vincent Montagnana